A Restoration

of the

Ancient Order of Things:

A Series of Articles by Alexander Campbell

Compiled and Edited by Jackson Erwin

Charleston, AR
COBB PUBLISHING
2023

Published in the United States by
Cobb Publishing
Charleston, AR
www.CobbPublishing.com
Editor@CobbPublishing.com

For more great Restoration Movement books, check out website!

ISBN: 978-1-960858-00-9

This work is dedicated to Alexander Campbell

"Through his faith, though he died, he still speaks."
Hebrews 11:4 (ESV)

Note About This Volume

This volume contains a series of thirty articles written by Campbell from Volumes 2–7 of the *Christian Baptist*. Each article's location has been recorded in the footnotes to assist the reader in referencing the original sources. However, the page numbers have not been provided for a few reasons:

First, we hope that this compilation will be used as a source by itself. This volume plans to make it easier for students and readers to find what Campbell wrote on theological matters quickly and effectively. Since the original locations of the articles have still been preserved, one can return to the original sources if he or she so desires.

Second, due to the number of reprintings the *Christian Baptist* and the *Millennial Harbinger* have gone through, and the variety of publishers over the years who have preserved these writings, providing the exact page numbers of these articles would be more of a hindrance than a help. In some of these reprints, the page numbers have changed—making it difficult to provide an *exact* reference for all students. However, we have kept the essentials for those who have access to the originals in case one needs to cite from them specifically.

One final point to clarify involves the text itself. These articles have been slightly edited to correct antiquated, misspelled, or misused words. However, this has been done as scarcely as possible. Scripture references have also been updated to suit modern readers.

Our hope is that this work will be an aid for those desiring to learn about Campbell's thoughts, and that Restoration students will aptly use these volumes as they progress in their studies of our reformation.

Table of Contents

Introduction

Alexander Campbell is a trademark name in the history of American Christianity. Regardless of one's theological perspective or background, Campbell has played a prominent role in evangelicalism and is worthy of much consideration. To some, he was a defender of the ancient faith, a reformer at heart, and a devout seeker of the truth. He questioned everything, whether good or bad, to ensure that his faith was substantiated by the Scriptures and reason.

Others have viewed Campbell as nothing more than a heretic—a deceiver responsible for leading millions away from reformed orthodoxy. He is believed to be a sectarian who created a new denomination based more upon Enlightenment ideals than the Bible. To them, he was not a proponent of restoration or reformation, but an entirely new system of thought labeled "Campbellism." That is, rather than bringing souls back to the old faith, he led them into something entirely new and different.

Still others—even within the Stone-Campbell Movement—have found fault in Campbell's work. On the right, it is believed that he did not go far enough in his reform. He is described as a ecumenical whose desire for Christian unity contradicted, and ultimately hindered, his goal of restoring the ancient order of things. On the left, he is seen as staunchly conservative and dangerously legalistic. His stance on the sufficiency of Scripture as the sole, infallible rule of faith is believed to be primitive, his writings on the role of women as sexist, and his views on mechanical instruments in worship as wrong-headed.

Surprisingly, these radically different perspectives on Campbell might work in his favor. Since he is viewed as both "far-right" and "far-left," the truth likely lies somewhere in between.

He was, perhaps, a balanced man in an imbalanced world. He was also a flawed man in a flawed world. Like all believers, he was prone to inconsistencies, ignorance, and at times arrogance.

Whatever biases one might hold toward Campbell, it is undeniable that he was a man of great intellect and motivation. In many ways, he carried an entire movement on his shoulders. He was a powerful instrument of God in helping form a Christian heritage that presently consists of a few million in the United States and millions more throughout the world. While one would be mistaken in assuming that Campbell was the founder of the movement and its fellowships (Disciples of Christ, Christian Churches, and Churches of Christ), others would be equally wrong in believing that he played a relatively small part in it. Had Campbell never been born, it is likely that this reformation never would have had the success it now enjoys.

Despite the vital role Campbell played in this tradition, many members within this fellowship know little to nothing about him. This is to our own detriment. Why? Because, by forgetting the men who labored before us, we consequently forget our own history, heritage, and vision. A major consequence of this historical drift is that, as the plea to unite Christendom on a plain and simple faith is forgotten, our purpose for existing is buried somewhere in the past. We appear as a people out of time, without a specific goal, and largely unaware of where our movement has been, is going, and needs to go.

The goal of this work is to resurrect the reforming spirit of Campbell. By reprinting his series of articles entitled *A Restoration of the Ancient Order of Things*, we hope to inspire and motivate our readers to learn from Campbell's example, sit at his feet, and examine his thoughts (with both their beauties and warts). These articles reveal the heart of Campbell as a reformer. In his desire to bring professing believers from all sects together,

Campbell knew that the only way such a feat could be accomplished was by embracing a simple, apostolic form of Christianity. One must be freed from the traditions and creeds of man that were added and bound to believers over the course of two millennia. Only then can the Christian truly be brought under the power of God's word as the sole rule of faith.

Christians often find themselves in agreement as to what the Bible teaches. Where we disagree, however, is in what the Bible *does not teach*. All Christians believe they are to sing, pray, have elders and deacons, and trust in the Person and work of Christ. However, we disagree about our creeds, expressions of worship, ecclesiastical councils, religious garbs, titles, and a host of other things. The mindset of reformers like Campbell was to keep what the Bible commands so we can unite and remove what is unnecessary (the so-called "non-essentials"), so we do not divide.

Hopefully, this volume will shed light on this great mind, and demonstrate why his teachings have resonated with so many believers in America and across the globe. Perhaps more interest will be garnered toward the Stone-Campbell Movement, and some of its principles brought into consideration.

Recommended Reading

Campbell, Selina. *Home Life and Reminiscences of Alexander Campbell*. St. Louis: John Burns, 1882.

Chalmers, Thomas. *Alexander Campbell's Tour in Scotland*. Nashville: Gospel Advocate, 1892.

Cobb, Bradley. *Alexander Campbell: A Collection*. 2 vols. Charleston, AR: Cobb Publishing, 2021.

Eames, S. Morris. *The Philosophy of Alexander Campbell*. Bethany, WV: Bethany College.

Humbert, Royal. *A Compend of Alexander Campbell's Theology*. St. Louis: Bethany Press, 1961.

Humble, Bill J. *Campbell and Controversy: The Debates of Alexander Campbell.* Joplin, MO: College Press, 1986.

Fitch, Alger M. *Alexander Campbell: Preacher of Reform and Reformer of Preaching.* Joplin, MO: College Press, 1988.

Foster, Douglas A. *A Life of Alexander Campbell.* Grand Rapids: Eerdmans, 2020.

Richardson, Robert. *Memoirs of Alexander Campbell.* Indianapolis, IN: Religious Book Service, 1897.

Chapter One

The Call to Restoration[1]

*Extract from the Minutes of the Baptist Missionary Association
of Kentucky, began and held at the Town-Fork Meetinghouse,
in Fayette County, on Saturday, the 11th of September, 1824.*

"The next meeting of this association will be in the first Baptist meetinghouse in Lexington, on the 30th of July next, which will be on the *fifth* Saturday of that month, at 11:00 A.M.

"It is proposed also to have a meeting of all the Baptist preachers who can attend, on Friday, the day preceding the meeting of the association, at 11:00 A.M. at the same place, for the purpose of *a general conference* on the state of religion, and on the subject of reform. All the ministers of the gospel in the Baptist denomination, favorable to these objects, are invited to attend, and, in the spirit of Christian love, by mutual counsel, influence, and exertion, according to the gospel, to aid in advancing the cause of piety in our state.

"*It is obvious to the most superficial observer, who is at all acquainted with the state of Christianity and of the church of the New Testament, that much, very much is wanting, to bring the Christianity and the church of the present day up to that standard — In what this deficiency consists, and how it is to be remedied, or whether it can be remedied at all, are the points to be discovered and determined.* In the deliberations intended, it is designed to take these subjects into serious consideration, and to report the result by way of suggestion and advisement to the Baptist Christian community, and to

---

[1] "A Restoration of the Ancient Order of Things — No. I," *Christian Baptist* Vol. 2, No. 7 (1825).

the churches to which the members of the meeting may particularly belong. We know very well that nothing can be done *right* which is not done according to the gospel or done *effectually* which is not done by the authority, and accompanied by the blessing of God. While God must do the work, we desire to know, and to acquiesce in his manner of doing it, and submissively to concur and obediently to go along with it."

The sentences we have *italicized* in the preceding extract, are sentences of no ordinary import. The first of them declares a truth as evident as a sunbeam in a cell, to all who have eyes to see. The second presents a subject of inquiry of paramount importance to all who expect to stand before the son of God in judgment. It affords us no common pleasure to see Christians awaking from their lethargic repose to the consideration of such subjects. That the fact should be acknowledged and lamented, that VERY MUCH IS WANTING TO BRING THE CHRISTIANITY AND THE CHURCH OF THE PRESENT DAY UP TO THE NEW TESTAMENT STANDARD amongst a people so intelligent, so respectable in numbers, and so influential, as the Baptist society in Kentucky; and that leaders of that community, so erudite, so pious, and so influential, should call upon their brethren to lay these things to heart, and to prepare themselves to make an effort towards reform, we hail as a most auspicious event.

As I feel deeply interested in every effort that is made, either amongst the Baptist or Paedo-Baptist societies, for the avowed object of reform, and as this subject has become familiar to my mind, from much reflection and a good deal of reading, I trust I shall not be considered as obtrusive in presenting a few remarks on the above extract, or rather in presenting certain thoughts, a favorable opportunity for which it presents.

Since the great *apostasy*, foretold and depicted by the holy apostles, attained to manhood's prime, or rather reached the awful climacteric, many *reformations* in religion have been attempted; some on a large and others on a more restricted scale. The page of history and the experience of the present generation concur in evincing that, *if any of those reformations began in the spirit, they have ended in the flesh.* This, indeed, may be as true of the reformers themselves as of their reformations. I believe, at the same time, that the reformers have themselves been benefactors, and their reformations benefits to mankind. I do cheerfully acknowledge, that all they who have been reputed reformers, have been our benefactors, and that we are all indebted to them in our political and religious capacities for their labors. Because they have not done everything which they might have done, or which they ought to have done, we should not withhold the need of thanks for what they have done. Although two systems of religion both end in the flesh, the one may be greatly preferable to the other. This will appear evident when it is considered that, amongst religious persecutors, some are more exorable and lenient than others. Now, if there should be two systems of religion that both lead to persecution and issue in it, that one which carries its rage no farther than to the prison and the whipping post, is greatly to be preferred to that which leads to the torturing wheel and to the faggot. The reason of this is very obvious, for most men would rather be whipped than burned for their religion. In other respects, there are differences, which are illustrated by the preceding.

Those reformers are not most deserving of our thanks which stand highest and most celebrated in the annals of reformations. We owe more to John Wickliffe than to Martin Luther, and more perhaps, to Peter Bruys than to John Calvin. The world is more indebted to Christopher Columbus than to Americus Vespusius, yet the latter supplanted the former in his well-earned fame. So

15

it has been amongst religious reformers. The success of every enterprise gives éclat to it. As great and as good men as George Washington have been hung or beheaded for treason.

The reformations most celebrated in the world are those which have departed the least from the systems they professed to reform. Hence, we have been often told that there is but a paper wall between England and Rome. The church of England, with king Henry or George IV as her head, though a celebrated reformation, has made but a few and very short strides from her mother, the church of Rome, with the pope at her head. So sensible of this are the good members of the reformed church of England, that they yet give to their king the title of *"Defender of the Faith,"* although the title was first given him by the pope for defending his faith. The reformation of the church of England, effected by Mr. Wesley, which issued in Episcopal Methodism, has entailed the same clerical dominion over that zealous people, which their forefathers complained of in the hierarchies of England and Rome. And not in England only does this dominion exist, but even in these United States, of all regions of the earth the most unfriendly to a religious monarchy, or even a religious oligarchy. The question remains yet to be decided, whether a *conference* of Methodist clergy, with its bishop in its chair, and laity at home, is any reformation at all from a *conclave* of English prelates, headed by a metropolitan or an archbishop. It is even uncertain whether the Methodist discipline has led more people to heaven, or made them happier on earth, than the rubric or liturgy of England.

All the famous reformations in history have rather been reformations of creeds and of clergy, than of religion. Since the New Testament was finished, it is fairly to be presumed that there cannot be any reformation of religion, properly so called. Though called reformations of religion, they have always left religion where it was. I do not think that king Henry was a whit more religious when he proclaimed himself head of the church of England, than when writing against Luther on the seven sacraments, as a true son of the church of Rome. It is even questionable whether Luther himself, the Elector of Saxony, the Marquis of Brandenburg, the Duke of Lunenburg, the Landgrave of Hesse, and the Prince of Anhalt, were more religious men when they signed the Augsburg *Confession of Faith*, than when they formerly repeated their *Ave Maria*.

Human creeds may be reformed and re-reformed, and be erroneous still, like their authors; but the inspired creed needs no reformation, being, like its author, infallible. The clergy, too, may be reformed from papistical opinions, grimaces, tricks, and dresses, to Protestant opinions and ceremonies; Protestant clergy may be reformed from Protestant to Presbyterial metaphysics and forms; and Presbyterian clergy may be reformed to Independency, and yet the Pope remain in their heart. They are clergy still—and still in need of reformation. Archbishop Laud and Lawrence Greatrake are both clergymen, though of different dimensions. The spirit of the latter is as lordly and as pontifical as that of the former, though his arm and his gown are shorter. The moschetta is an animal of the same genus with the hornet, though the bite of the former is not so powerful as the sting of the latter. A creed, too, that is formed in Geneva or in London, is as *human* as one formed in Rome or Constantinople. They have all given employment to tax-gatherers, jail-keepers, and gravediggers.

All reformations in religious opinions and speculations have been fated like the fashions in apparel. They have lived, and died, and revived, and died again. As apparel has been the badge of rank, so have opinions been the badge of parties, and the cause of their rise and continuance. The green and orange ribbon, as well as the blue stocking, have been as useful and as honorable to those that have worn them, as those opinions were to the possessors, which have been the shibboleths of religious parties.

Human systems, whether of philosophy or of religion, are proper subjects of reformation; but Christianity cannot be reformed. Every attempt to reform Christianity is like an attempt to create a new sun, or to change the revolutions of the heavenly bodies--unprofitable and vain. In a word we have had reformations enough. The very name has become as offensive as the term *"Revolution"* in France.

A RESTORATION *of the ancient order of things* is all that is necessary to the happiness and usefulness of Christians. No attempt "to reform the doctrine, discipline and government of the church," (a phrase too long in use) can promise a better result that those which have been attempted and languished unto death. We are glad to see, in the above extract, that the thing proposed, is to bring the Christianity and the church of the present day up to the standard of the New Testament.

This is in substance, though in other terms, what we contend for. To bring the societies of Christians *up* to the New Testament, is just to bring the disciples, individually and collectively, to walk in the faith, and in the commandments of the Lord and Savior, as presented in that blessed volume; and this is to *restore* the ancient order of things. Celebrated as the *era of Reformation* is, we doubt not but that the *era of Restoration* will as far transcend it in importance and fame, through the long and blissful Millennium, as the New Testament transcends in simplicity, beauty, excellency, and majesty, the dogmas and notions of the creed of Westminster and the canons of the Assembly's Digest. Just in so far as the ancient order of things, or the religion of the New Testament, is restored, just so far has the Millennium commenced, and so far has its blessings been enjoyed. For, to the end of time, we shall have no other revelation of the Spirit, no other New Testament, no other Savior, and no other religion than we now have, when we understand, believe, and practice the doctrine of Christ delivered unto us by his apostles.

Chapter Two

Unity and the Usage of Creeds[2]

Had the founder of the Christian faith been defective in wisdom or benevolence, then his authority, his testimony, and his commandments, might be canvassed with as little ceremony as the discoveries and maxims of our compeers and cotemporaries; then his religion might be improved, or reformed, or better adapted to existing circumstances. But as all Christians admit that he foresaw and anticipated all the events and revolutions in human history, and that the present state of things was as present to his mind as the circumstances that encompassed him in Judea, or in the judgment hall of Caiaphas; that he had wisdom and understanding perfectly adequate to institute, arrange, and adapt a system of things, suitable to all exigencies and emergencies of men and things, and that his philanthropy was not only unparalleled in the annals of the world, but absolutely perfect, and necessarily leading to, and resulting in, that institution of religion which was most beneficial to man in the present and future world. I say, all these things being generally, if not universally agreed upon by all Christians, then it follows, by the plainest and most certain consequence, that the institution of which he is the author and founder, can never be either improved or reformed. The lives or conduct of his disciples may be reformed, but his religion cannot. The religion of Rome, or of England, or of Scotland may be reformed, but the religion of Jesus Christ never can. When we have found ourselves out of the way we

---

[2] "A Restoration of the Ancient Order of Things — No. II," *Christian Baptist* Vol. 2, No. 8 (1825).

may seek for the ancient paths, but we are not at liberty to invent paths for our own feet. We should return unto the Lord.

But *a restoration of the ancient order of things,* it appears, is all that is contemplated by the wise disciples of the Lord, as it is agreed that this is all that is wanting to the perfection, happiness, and glory of the Christian community. To contribute to this is our most ardent desire — our daily and diligent inquiry and pursuit. Now, in attempting to accomplish this, it must be observed, that it belongs to every individual and to every congregation of individuals to discard from their faith and their practice everything that is not found written in the New Testament of the Lord and Savior, and to believe and practice whatever is there enjoined. This done, and everything is done which ought to be done.

But to come to the things to be discarded, we observe that, in the ancient order of things, there were no creeds or compilations of doctrine in abstract terms, nor in other terms other than the terms adopted by the Holy Spirit in the New Testament. *Therefore, all such are to be discarded.* It is enough to prove that they ought to be discarded, from the fact that none of those now in use, nor ever at any time in use, existed in the apostolic age, but as many considerations are urged why they should be used, we shall briefly advert to these, and attempt to show that they are perfectly irrational, and consequently foolish and vain.

I.

It is argued that confessions of faith are or may be much plainer and of much more easy apprehension and comprehension than the oracles of God. Men, then, are either wiser or more benevolent than God. If the truths in the Bible can be expressed more plainly by modern divines than they are by the Holy Spirit, then it follows that either God *would not* or *could not* express them in words so plainly as man. If he *could,* and *would not,* express them in words so suitable as men employ, then he is less benevolent than they. Again, if he *would,* but *could not* express them in words so suitable as men employ, then he is not so wise as they. These conclusions, we think, are plain and unavoidable. We shall thank any advocate of human creeds to attempt to show any way of escaping this dilemma.

But the abstract and metaphysical dogmas of the best creeds now extant, are the most difficult of apprehension and comprehension. They are farther from the comprehension of nine-tenths of mankind than the words employed by the Holy Spirit. We shall give a few samples from the Westminster creed, one of the best in the world: —

Sample 1. "The Father is of none, neither begotten nor proceeding; the Son is eternally begotten of the Father; the Holy Ghost eternally proceeding from the Father and the Son."

Sample 2. "God, from all eternity, did, by the most wise and holy counsel of his own will, freely and unchangeably ordain whatsoever comes to pass; yet so as neither is God the Author of sin, nor is violence offered to the will of the creatures, nor is the liberty or contingency of second causes taken away, but rather established."

Sample 3. "Although God knows whatsoever may or can come to pass, upon all supposed conditions; yet hath he not decreed anything because he foresaw it as future, or as that which would come to pass upon such conditions."

Sample 4. "These angels and men, thus predestinated and foreordained, are particularly and unchangeably designed, and their number is so certain and definite, that it cannot be either increased or diminished."

Sample 5. "Although in relation to the knowledge and decree of God, the first cause, all things come to pass immutably and infallibly; yet, by the same providence, he ordereth them to fall out according to the nature of second causes, either necessarily, freely, or contingently."

These samples are taken out of chapters 2, 3, and 5, and may serve as a fair specimen of the whole. Now the question is whether are these words more plainly, definitely, and intelligibly expressive of divine truths than the terms used by the Holy Spirit in the Scriptures? We do not ask the question, whether these *things* are taught in the Bible? but merely whether *these terms* are more plain, definite, and intelligible than the terms used in the Bible? This we refer to the reader's own decision.

II.

But, in the second place, it is argued that human confession of faith is necessary to *the unity* of the church. If they are *necessary* to the unity of the church, then the church cannot be united and one without them. But the church of Christ was united and one in all Judea, in the first age, without them; therefore, they are not *necessary* to the unity of the church. But again, if they are *necessary* to the unity of the church, then the New Testament is defective; for if the New Testament was sufficient to the unity of the church, then human creeds would not be necessary. If any man, therefore, contend that human creeds are *necessary* to the unity of the church, he at the same time, and by *all the same arguments,* contends that the scriptures of the Holy Spirit are insufficient — that is, imperfect or defective. Every human creed is predicated upon the inadequacy, that is, the imperfection of the Holy Scriptures.

But the records of all religious sects, and the experience of all men of observation, concur in attesting the fact that human creeds have contributed always, since their first introduction, to divide and disunite the professors of the Christian religion.[3]

Every attempt to found the unity of the church upon the adoption of any creed of human device, is not only incompatible with the nature and circumstances of mankind, but is an effort to frustrate or to defeat the prayer of the Lord Messiah, and to subvert his throne and government. This sentence demands some attention. We shall illustrate and establish the truth which it asserts.

Human creeds are composed of the inferences of the human understanding speculating upon the revelation of God. Such are all those now extant. The inferences drawn by the human understanding partake of all the defects of that understanding. Thus, we often observe two men sincerely exercising their mental powers upon the same words of inspiration, drawing inferences or conclusions, not only diverse, but flatly contradictory. This is the result of a variety of circumstances. The prejudices of education, habits of thinking, modes of reasoning, different degrees of information, the influence of a variety of passions and interests, and, above all, the different degrees of strength of human intellect, all concur in producing this result. The persons themselves are very often unconscious of the operation of all these circumstances, and are, therefore, honestly and sincerely zealous in believing and in maintaining the truth of their respective conclusions. These conclusions, then, are always private property, and can never be placed upon a level with the inspired word. Subscription to them, or an acknowledgement of them, can never be rationally required as a *bond of union*. If, indeed, all Christians

---

[3] "The confirmation of this we shall reserve to another time, when it will be convenient to introduce a detail of historical facts. In our next number we intend to give a brief and faithful compend of the history of the formation of the Westminster Creed, from a source that cannot be questioned."

were alike in all those circumstantial differences already mentioned, then an accordance in all the conclusions which one or more of them might draw from the divine volume, might rationally be expected from them all. But as Christians have never yet all possessed the same prejudices, degrees of information, passions, interests, modes of thinking and reasoning, and the same strength of understanding, an attempt to associate them under the banners of a human creed composed of human inferences, and requiring unanimity in the adoption of it, is every way as irrational as to make a uniformity of features, of color, of height, and weight, a bond of union. A society of this kind never yet existed, and we may, I think, safely affirm, never will. Those societies which unite upon the 39 articles of the Church of England, and the 33 chapters of the Kirk of Scotland, do not heartily concur in those creeds. Most of them never read them, few of them examine them, and still fewer heartily concur in yielding the same credence, or in reposing the same confidence in them.

Their being held as a *nominal bond of union,* gives rise to hypocrisy, prevarication, lying, and, in many instances, to the basest injustice. Many men are retained in those communities who are known not to approbate them fully, to have exceptions and objections; but their wealth or some extrinsic circumstance palliates their non-conformities in opinion; whereas others are reproached, persecuted, and expelled, who differ no more than they, but there is some interest to consult, some pique, or resentment, or envy to gratify in their excommunication. This is base injustice. Many, like the late Rev. Dr. Scott, subscribe them for preferment. He declared that he was moved by the Holy Spirit to enter into the ministry, and yet he afterwards avowed that then he did not believe there was any Holy Spirit. This is lying and hypocrisy. These are, however, incidental occurrences. But the number of such cases, and the frequency of their occurrence, are alarming to those who believe that God reigns. Again, the number of items which enter into those creeds is not amongst the least of their absurdities. In the Presbyterian Confession there are thirty-three chapters, and in these one hundred and seventy-one dogmas. In receiving "ministers," or in "licensing preachers," it is ordained that the candidate be asked, "Do *you sincerely receive and adopt the Confession of Faith of this church, as containing the system of doctrine taught in the Holy Scriptures?"* Observe the words, *"the system."* Yes, the identical *system* taught in the Scriptures—that is, the 171 dogmas of the Confession is *the system* of truth taught in the Holy Scriptures. Neither more nor less! But I am digressing. I only proposed in this place to show that the imposition of any creed of human device is incompatible with the nature and circumstances of man. This, I conceive, is rendered sufficiently plain from an inspection of the circumstances and character of the human mind already noticed.

But it was affirmed, that every attempt to found the unity of the church upon the adoption of any creed of human contrivances; – upon any creed, other than the apostle's testimony, is not only incompatible with the nature and circumstances of mankind, but is also an effort to frustrate and defeat the prayer and plan of the Lord Messiah, and to subvert his throne and government.

It will be confessed, without argument to prove, that the conversion of men, or of the world, and the unity, purity, and happiness of the disciples of the Messiah, were the sublime subjects of his humiliation unto death. For this he prayed in language never heard on earth before, in words which not only expressed the ardency of his desires, but at the same time unfolded the *plan* in which his benevolence and philanthropy were to be triumphant.

The words to which we refer express one petition of that prayer recorded by the apostle John, commonly styled his intercessory prayer. With his eyes raised to heaven, he says; — "Holy

Father — now, I do not pray for these only (for the unity and success of the apostles) but for those also who shall believe on me through, or by means of *their* word — that THEY ALL MAY BE ONE, — THAT THE WORLD MAY BELIEVE THAT THOU HAST SENT ME." Who does not see in this petition, that the words or testimony of the apostles, the unity of the disciples, and the conviction of the world are bound together by the wisdom and the love of the Father, by the devotion and philanthropy of the Son. The order of heaven, the plan of the Great King, his throne and government, are here unfolded in full splendor to our view. The *words of the apostles* are laid as the basis, *the unity of the disciples* the glorious result, and the only successful means of converting the world to the acknowledgement, that Jesus of Nazareth is the Messiah or the Son of the Blessed, the only Savior of men.

Let us attend to the argument of the prayer. The *will* of Jesus was the same as the will of him who sent him. The will of heaven, that is, the will of the Father, and of the Son, and of the Holy Spirit, is, that all who believe on the Messiah through the testimony of the apostles may be one; consequently, they do not will that those who believe on him through the Westminster divines shall be one. The words of the prayer alone demonstrate this. And who does not see, and who will not confess, that the fact proves, the fact now existing, that those who believe in him through the words of the Westminster divines are not one? They are cut up or divided into seven sects at this moment. While the Savior prays that those who believe on him through the apostles may be one, he in fact, and in the plain meaning of terms, prays that they who believe on him through any other media or means may be divided, and not be one.

To attempt to unite the professing disciples by any other means than the word of the apostles, by the Westminster, or any other creed, is, then, an attempt to overrule the will of heaven, to subvert the throne of the Great King, to frustrate the prayers of the Son of the Blessed. As the heavens are higher than the earth, so are God's thoughts and ways higher than ours. He knows, for he has willed, and planned, and determined, that neither the Popish, the Protestant, the Presbyterian, the Methodist, nor the Baptist creed shall be honored more than the apostle's testimony, shall be honored as much as the apostle's testimony, shall be honored at all. These creeds the Savior proscribed forever; they are rebellion against his plan and throne, and they are aimed at the dethronement of the Holy Twelve—He put *them* on thrones, he gave them this honor. All creed makers have disputed their right to the throne, have attempted, *ipso facto,*[4] their degradation, and have usurped their government. But he that sits in heaven has laughed at them, he has vexed them in his sore displeasure, he has dispersed them in his anger, and confounded their language as he did their predecessors, who sought to subvert his throne and dominion by the erection of a *tower* and citadel reaching to the skies. The votaries of those creed makers have also concurred with their masters and have attempted to raise them upon their shoulders to the apostolic thrones; but he has broken their necks, and they go bowed down always. He has made them lick the dust and caused children to reign over them.

But the conversion of the world is planned and ordered by the will of heaven to be dependent on the unity of the disciples, as well as this unity dependent upon the apostle's testimony. An attempt to convert Pagans and Muslims to believe that Jesus is the Son of God, and *the sent* of the Father, until Christians are united, is also an attempt to frustrate the prayer of the Messiah, to subvert his throne and government. There are unalterable laws in the moral world, as in the natural. There are also unalterable laws in the government of the moral and religious world,

---

[4] Or, "by the very fact or act."

as in the government of the natural. Those laws cannot, by human interference, be set aside or frustrated—We might as reasonably expect that Indian corn will grow in the open fields in the midst of the frost and snows of winter, as that Pagan nations can be converted to Jesus Christ, till Christians are united through the belief of the apostle's testimony. We may force corn to grow by artificial means in the depth of winter, but it is not like the corn of August. So may a few disciples be made in Pagan lands by such means in the moral empire; as those by which corn is made to grow in winter in the natural empire, but they are not like the disciples of primitive times before sectarian creeds came into being. It is enough to say, on this topic, that the Savior made *the unity of the disciples* essential to the conviction of the world; and he that attempts it independent of this essential, sets himself against the wisdom and plans of heaven, and aims at overruling the dominion and government of the Great King. On this subject we have many things to say, and hard to be uttered, because the people are dull of hearing. But we shall leave this prayer for the present, having just introduced it, and noticed the argument of it, by reminding the reader that instead of human creeds, promoting the *unity* of the disciples, they have always operated just the reverse; and are in diametrical opposition to the wisdom and benevolence of the Heavens. Should the Christian community be united upon the Westminster, or Methodist, or Baptist, or any human creed, then the plan of heaven is defeated, the apostles disgraced, the Savior's prayer unanswered, and the whole order of heaven frustrated, and the throne of the universe subverted. He that advocates the *necessity* of creeds of human contrivance *to the unity of the church* unconsciously impeaches the wisdom of God, arraigns the benevolence of the Savior, and censures the revelation of the Spirit. He, perhaps, without reflection attempts to newly modify the empire of reason, of morality and religion; to rise above, not only the apostles, but the Savior himself, and

arrogates to himself a wisdom and philanthropy that far sur-
passes, and in fact covers with disgrace, all those attributes that
rise to our view, and shine with incomparable effulgence in the
redemption of man.

Chapter Three

Unity, Creeds, and Conversion Experience[5]

"HOLY FATHER—now I do not pray for these only, but for those also who shall believe on me THROUGH THEIR WORD, *that they all may be* ONE—That THE WORLD MAY BELIEVE *that thou hast sent me.*" The testimony of the apostles, the Savior makes the grand means of the enlargement and consolidation of his empire. He prays that they who believe on him through their testimony may be united. And their union he desires, that the world may believe that he was sent of God, and acted under the authority, and according to the will of the God and Father of all. The word of the apostles, the unity of those who believe it, and the conviction of the world are here inseparably associated. All terminate in the conviction of the world. As the Father so loved the world that he gave his only begotten Son; as the Son so loved the world as to become a propitiation for its sins, and as the Spirit came to convince the world of sin, of righteousness and of judgment, the conviction of the world is an object of the dearest magnitude in the estimation of the Heavens. All the attributes of Deity require that this grand object be achieved in a certain way, or not at all. That way or plan the Savior has unfolded in his address from earth to heaven. We all must confess, however reluctant at first, that, in the government of the world, there are certain ways to certain ends, and if not accomplished in this way they are not accomplished at all. The fact is apparent, and most obvious, whether we understand, or can understand the reason of it. As well might Israel have dispossessed the Canaanites in

---

[5] "A Restoration of the Ancient Order of Things—No. III," *Christian Baptist* Vol. 2, No. 9 (1825).

any other way he might have devised, as we attempt to carry any point against the established order of Heaven. Israel failed in his own way; in God's way he was successful. We have failed in our own way to convince the world, but in God's way we would be victorious. Wisdom and benevolence combined constitute his plan, and although his ways may appear weak or incomprehensible, they are, in their moral grandeur of wisdom and benevolence, as much higher than ours, as the heavens are higher than the earth.

For anything we know, it was in the bounds of possibilities for the Savior to have founded his kingdom without apostles or their word; but we are assured, from the fact of their having been employed, that his wisdom and benevolence required, in reference to things on earth and things in heaven, that they should be employed. If then, as is evident, there is a certain way in which Christianity can pervade the world, and if the unity of the disciples is an essential constituent of this way, how grievous the schisms, how mischievous the divisions amongst them! While they are contending about their orthodoxy and their heterodoxies, they are hardening the hearts of the unbelievers at home, and shutting the door of faith against the nations abroad. While the Savior, in the prospects of all the sorrows that were about to environ him, in the greatness of his philanthropy, forgetful and regardless of them all, was pouring out his fervent desires for the oneness of his followers, many that call themselves his disciples are fomenting new divisions, or strenuously engaged in keeping up the old ones. They in fact prefer their paltry notions, their abstract devices, their petty *shibboleths* to the conversion of the world. Yes, as one of the regenerate divines said, some time since, he would as soon have communion with thieves and robbers, as with those who disputed his notions about eternal generation, or eternal procession, or some such metaphysical nonsense; so, many, in appearance, would rather that the world should continue in Pagan darkness for a thousand years, than that they should give up with a dogmatic confession, without a life giving truth in it.[6] From the Roman pontiff down to a licensed beneficiary, each high priest and Levite labors to build up the shibboleths of a party. With every one of them, his cause, that brings him a morsel of bread, is the cause of God. Colleges are founded, acts of incorporation prayed for as sincerely as the Savior prayed for the union of Christians in order to the conversion of the world, theological schools erected, and a thousand contributions levied for keeping up parties and rewarding their leaders.

I have no idea of seeing, nor one wish to see the sects unite in one grand army. This would be dangerous to our liberties and laws. For this the Savior did not pray. It is only the disciples of Christ dispersed amongst them, that reason and benevolence would call out of them. Let them unite who love the Lord, and then we shall soon see the hireling priesthood and their worldly establishments prostrate in the dust.

But creeds of human contrivance keep up these establishments, nay, they are declared by some sects to be their very constitution. These create, and foster, and mature that state of things which operates against the letter and spirit of the Savior's prayer. The disciples cannot be united while these are recognized; and while these are not one, the world cannot be converted. So far from being the bond of union, or the means of uniting the saints, they are the bones of controversy, the seeds of discord, the cause as well as the effect of division. As reasonably might we expect the articles of confederation that league the "Holy Alliance" to be the constitution of a republic, as that the

---

[6] "The history of the world has not informed me of one sinner brought to repentance or converted unto Jesus Christ by any confession of faith in existence."

35

Westminster or any other creed should become a means of uniting Christians. It may for a time hold together a worldly establishment and be of the same service as an act of incorporation to a Presbyterian congregation, which enables it to make the unwilling *willing* to pay their stipends, but by and by it becomes a scorpion even amongst themselves.

But the constitution of the kingdom of the Savior is the New Testament, and this alone is adapted to the existence of his kingdom in the world. *To restore the ancient order of things* this must be recognized as the only constitution of this kingdom. And in receiving citizens they must be received into the kingdom, just as they were received by the apostles into it, when they were in the employment of setting it up. And here let us ask, how did they receive them? Did they propose any articles of religious opinions? Did they impose any inferential principles, or require the acknowledgment of any dogmas whatever? Not one. *The acknowledgment of the king's supremacy in one proposition expressive of a fact, and not an opinion, and a promise of allegiance expressed in the act of naturalization, were every item requisite to all the privileges of citizenship.* As this is a fundamental point, we shall be more particular in detail.

When any person desired admission into the kingdom, he was only asked what he thought of the king. "Dost thou believe in thine heart that Jesus of Nazareth is the Messiah, the Lord of all," was the whole amount of the apostolic requirement. If the candidate for admission replied in the affirmative—if he declared his hearty conviction of this fact—no other interrogation was proposed. They took him on his solemn declaration of this belief, whether Jew or Gentile, without a single demur. He was forthwith naturalized, and formally declared to be a citizen of the kingdom of Messiah. In the act of naturalization, which was *then* performed by means of water, he abjured or renounced spiritual allegiance to any other prince, potentate, pontiff, or

36

prophet, than Jesus the Lord. He was then treated by the citizens as a fellow-citizen of the saints and invited to the religious festivals of the brotherhood. And whether he went to Rome, Antioch, or Ephesus, he was received and treated by all the subjects of the Great King as a brother and fellow citizen. If he ever exhibited any instances of disloyalty, he was affectionately reprimanded; but if he was guilty of treason against the King, he was simply excluded from the kingdom. But we are now speaking of the constitutional admission of citizens into the kingdom of Jesus Christ, and not of anything subsequent thereunto. The declaration of the belief of one fact, expressed in one plain proposition, and the one act of naturalization, constituted a free citizen of this kingdom. Such was the ancient order of things, as all must confess. Why, then, should we adopt a new plan, of our own devising, which, too, is as irrational as unconstitutional?

Let me here ask the only people in our land who seem to understand the constitution of our kingdom and the laws of our King in these respects, why do you, my Baptist brethren, in receiving applicants into the kingdom, ask them so many questions about matters and things which the apostles never dreamt of, before you will permit them to be naturalized? Although you do not, like some others, present a book for their acknowledgment, you do that which is quite as unauthorized and as unconstitutional.

Your applicant is importuned in the presence of a congregation who sit as jurors upon his case, to tell *how*, and *why*, and *wherefore* he is moved to seek for admission into the kingdom. He is now to tell "what the Lord has done for his soul, what he felt, and how he was awakened, and how he now feels," etc. After he has told his "experience," some of the jurors interrogate him for their own satisfaction; and, among other abstract metaphysics, he is asked such questions as the following: "Did you not feel as though you deserved to be sent to hell for your sins?

Did you not see that God would be just in excluding you from his presence forever? Did you not view sin as an infinite evil? Do you not now take delight in the things which were once irksome to you?" etc. If his responses coincide with the experience and views of his examiners, his experience is pronounced genuine. He not unfrequently tells of something like Paul's visions and revelations, which give a sort of variety to his accounts, which, with some, greatly prove the genuineness of his conversion.[7] Now what is all this worth? His profession is not that which the apostles required; and the only question is whether the apostolic order of this is the wiser, happier, and safer. When the eunuch said, "Here is water, what doth hinder me to be baptized?" Philip said, "If thou believest with all thine heart, thou mayest." He replied, *"I believe that Jesus Christ is the Son of God."* Philip then accompanied him into the water and immersed him. None of your questions were propounded — no congregation was assembled to judge of his experience. Philip, as all his contemporaries

---

[7] "The reader may, perhaps, think that we speak too irreverently of the practice and of the experience of many Christians. We have no such intention. But there are many things when told or represented just as they are, which appear so strange, and, indeed, fanciful, that the mere recitation of them assumes an air of irony. I confess, upon the whole, that this order of things appears to me as unreasonable and as novel as the following case: —James Sanitas once had a consumption. By a few simples, a change of air, and exercise, he recovered his former good health. He was importuned by Thomas Medicus, a physician, to converse about his former disease and recovery. The Doctor doubted whether he was really restored to health. He asked what medicines he used. James Sanitas replied. The Doctor asked him whether he felt an acute pain in his breast or side for so long a time. He next inquired if certain simples were used, and how they operated. Last of all he inquired hat his present feelings were. The answers of James did not correspond with Dr. Medicus' theory and was told that he had still the same malady and was in circumstances as dangerous as before. James assured him he felt perfectly sound and vigorous, and appealed to the manifest change in his appearance, corpulency, color, strength, etc. The Doctor settled the controversy by telling him that unless he felt certain pains so long, and a peculiar class of sensations while using the simples prescribed, he is deceived, he cannot be cured, he is yet consumptive, and must die."

did, took him on his word. Now I think, brethren, that you cannot say I assume too much when I declare my conviction that the apostolic method was better than yours. You object that a person's *saying* he believes what the eunuch believed does not afford you sufficient evidence to disciple him. Well, we shall hear you. But let me ask, if he heartily believe what the eunuch believed, is he not worthy of baptism? "Yes," I hear you respond. Now for his *saying* he believes. What have you but his *saying* that he feels or felt what he described as his experience? You take his word in that case when accompanied with manifest sincerity. Why not, then, take his word in this case when accompanied with manifest sincerity? Yes, but say you, any person can learn to say that he believes what the eunuch believed. Admitted. What then? Cannot any person who has heard others catechized or examined for his experience, *learn* too to describe what he never felt? So far, the cases are perfectly equal. The same assurance is given in both cases. You take the applicant on his own testimony — so did they. We both depend upon his word, and we grant he may deceive us, and you know he has often deceived you. But we could easily show, were it our intention, that you are more liable to be deceived than we. But we leave this and ask for no more than what is abundantly evident, that the apostolic plan affords the same assurance as yours. We have the word of the applicant, and you have no more. These considerations show that the apostolic plan is the wiser and the safer. It is more honorable to the truth too. It fixes the attention of all upon the magnitude of the gospel faith — upon the magnitude of the fact confessed. It exalts it in the apprehension of all as the most grand, sublime, and all-powerful fact. It makes it to the disciple, in his views, what the Savior is in all the counsels of God — the *Alpha* and the *Omega*. It shows its comprehensive and fundamental import, which in fact transcends every other consideration. Moreover, *the disciple thus baptized is baptized into the faith*, but in the modern plan he is *baptized into his own experience.* It is then most honorable to the saving truth.

"But," says one, "you may soon get many applicants in this way." Stop, my friend, I fear not so many. You will, if you interrogate the people, find many to say they believe what the eunuch believed, but you cannot persuade them to do as the eunuch did. They will confess with their mouth this truth, but they do not wish to be naturalized or to put themselves under the constitution of the Great King. Their not *moving* in obedience proves the truth does not *move them.* But when any person asks what the eunuch asked, he, *ipso facto,*[8] shows that his faith has moved him, and this authorized Philip to comply with his desires, and should induce us to go and do likewise. When the ancient order of things is restored, neither more nor less will be demanded of any applicant for admission into the kingdom, than was asked by Philip. And every man who solicits admission in this way — who solemnly declares that, upon the testimony and authority of the holy apostles and prophets, he believes that Jesus is the Messiah, the Son of the living God, should forthwith be baptized without respect to any questions or dogmas derived either from written creeds or church covenants. But I have wandered far from my investigation of the merits of the arguments in favor of creeds — so far that I cannot approach them until my next.

---

[8] Or, "by the very fact or act."

Chapter Four

Words of the Apostles as the Only Christian Creed [9]

That the *word of the apostles* shall be the only creed, formula, and directory of faith, worship, and Christian practice, when the ancient order of things is restored, we have offered some evidence to show. The constitution and law of the primitive church shall be the constitution and law of the restored church. As the constitution and law then admitted all the faithful disciples of the Lord to an equal participation of all privileges; so, when the same is again adopted, the same privileges will be extended to every orderly citizen of the kingdom. Without any of our modern creeds in substance or in form the church was once united, complete, and happy, and will be so again. For the same cause will always produce the same effect. When the disciples shall return to the Lord, he will return unto them.

In receiving members or citizens into the kingdom, or in naturalizing foreigners, it appeared, in our last essay, that nothing was required of them but an acknowledgment of the word or testimony of the witnesses concerning the King, Jesus of Nazareth. A hearty declaration, or confession with their lips, that they believed in their hearts, that Jesus of Nazareth was the Messiah, the Son of the living God, the King and Lord of all, qualified them as applicants for naturalization. In the act of immersion into this name, they renounced every other Messiah, Lord, King, or Savior; they put off their former religion, and renounced every religious obligation to any other system or authority, *and put on Jesus*, as their Lord and King. From a consideration of the

---

[9] "A Restoration of the Ancient Order of Things — No. IV," *Christian Baptist* Vol. 2, No. 11 (1825).

ancient order it appeared, that the apostles did not command men to be baptized *into their own experience,* but *into the faith then delivered to the saints.* It was affirmed that the ancient order was *wise, safer,*[10] and *more honorable to the saving truth, than the modern way of receiving members into a Baptist society, and some proof was presented.*

In the present essay we shall make a few remarks upon another important preliminary to the restoration of the ancient order of things. *There must be, and there shall be an abandonment of the new and corrupt nomenclature, and a restoration of the inspired one.* In other words, there must be an abandonment of the Babylonish or corrupt phraseology of the dark ages and of modern discoveries, in the fixed style of the Christian vocabulary. This is a matter of greater importance than may, at first sight, appear to all. Words and names long consecrated, and sanctified by long prescription, have a very imposing influence upon the human understanding. We think as well as speak by means of words. It is just as impossible for an adult to think as to speak without words. Let him that doubts make the experiment. Now as all correct ideas of God and things invisible are supernatural ideas, no other terms can so suitably express them as the terms adopted by the Holy Spirit, in adapting those supernatural truths to our apprehension. He that taught man to speak, would, doubtless adopt the most suitable terms in his language to reveal himself to his understanding. To disparage those terms, by adopting others in preference, is presumptuous and insolent on the part of man. Besides, when men adopt terms to express supernatural truths, it is not the truths themselves, but their ideas of them they communicate. They select such terms as suit their apprehensions of revealed truth, and hence the terms they use are expressive

---

[10] "The following paragraph was left out of the last number by an oversight of the printer. It was in demonstration that the apostolic order was the safer."

only of their conceptions of divine things and must just be as imperfect as their conceptions are. It is impossible for any man, unless by accident, to express accurately that which he apprehends imperfectly. From this source springs most of our *doctrinal* controversies—Men's opinions, expressed in their own terms, are often called Bible truths. In order then to a full restoration of the ancient order of things there must be "a pure speech" restored. And I think the Lord once said, in order to a restoration, that he would restore to the people "a pure speech." We know that the ancient order of things amongst the Jews, could not be restored, after their captivity in Babylon, until the law of the Lord, containing the primitive institutions of the Jews' religion, was read and understood by the people, and the dialect of Babylon abandoned as far as it corrupted the primitive simplicity of that religion. Hence the scribes read them the law from morning to evening, gave them the sense and made them understand the reading. This became necessary because of the corrupt dialect they had learned in Babylon, on account of which their revelation was unintelligible to them until the language of Canaan was purged from the phraseology of Ashdod. It will, we apprehend, be found precisely similar in the antitype, or in the return of the people of God from the captivity of Babylon the great, the mother of abominations.

But we shall go on to specify a sample of those Babylonish terms and phrases which must be purged from the Christian vocabulary, before the saints can understand the religion they profess, or one another as fellow disciples. I select these from the approved standards of the most popular establishments. For from these they have become current and sacred style. Such are the following—"Trinity. First, second, and third person in the adorable Trinity God the Son; and God the Holy Ghost. Eternal Son. The Son is eternally begotten of the Father; the Holy Ghost eternally proceeding from the Father and the Son. The divinity of Jesus Christ; the humanity of Jesus Christ; the incarnation of Jesus Christ. This he said as man; and that as God. The common operations, and the special operations of the Spirit of God. Original sin, and original righteousness. Spiritual death; spiritual life. Covenant of works, covenant of grace, and covenant of redemption; a dispensation of the covenant of grace, and administration of the covenant. Effectual calling. Free will. Free Grace. Total depravity. Eternal justification. Eternal sheep. Elect world. Elect infants. Light of nature. Natural religion. General and particular atonement. Legal and evangelical repentance. Moral, ceremonial, and judicial law. Under the law as a covenant of works, and as a rule of life. Christian Sabbath. Holy sacrament. Administration of the sacrament. Different kinds of faith and grace. Divine service; the public worship of God, etc."

These are but a mere sample, and all of one species. It will be said that men cannot speak of Bible truths without adopting other terms than those found in the written word. This will be granted, and yet there will be found no excuse for the above species of unauthorized and Babylonish phraseology. It is one thing to speak *of* divine truths in our own language, and another to adopt a *fixed style of expressing* revealed truths to the exclusion of, or in preference to, that fixed by the Spirit, and sometimes, too, at variance with it. For instance, the terms Trinity, first and second person of — Eternal Son, and the eternal procession of the Spirit, are now the fixed style in speaking of God, his Son Jesus Christ, and of the Spirit, in reference to their "Personal Character." Now this is not the style of the oracles of God. It is all human and may be as freely criticized as one of the numbers of the Spectator. Yet because of the sanctified character of these terms, having been baptized, or authorized by the orthodox and pious for centuries, it is at the risqué of my reputation for orthodoxy, and at the expense of being charged with heresy, that I simply affirm that they are terms that the wisdom of this world teacheth, and not the Spirit of God. I would not be startled to hear that I have denied the faith and rejected the revealed character of the Father, Son, and Holy Spirit, because I have said that the fixed style in speaking of them in the popular establishments is of human origin and of the language of Ashdod, and not of the language of Canaan. This, however, only proves that the terms of human philosophy are held as sacred, or rather more sacred, than the words of the Holy Spirit.

These terms originate new doctrines. Thus, the term "trinity" gives rise to the *doctrine of the trinity*. And what fierce controversies have originated out of this doctrine! How many creeds and martyrs has it made! Courteous and pious reader, would it not be as wise, as humble, and as modest too, for us, on such topics, to prefer the words of the Holy Spirit, and to speak of God, his Son, and Spirit, as the apostles did. Moreover, these terms do not help our conceptions of God at all. They rather impede than facilitate our understanding the divine oracles. It is not more difficult to conceive of an eternal Son eternally begotten, and of a Spirit eternally proceeding, than to understand anything God has ever spoken to men. And see on what slender thread those distinctions hang. Because Jesus Christ told his disciples that he would *send* them the Spirit, which Spirit *would* or *was to proceed* from his Father, or to be *sent forth* by his Father as well as by himself; therefore, the schoolmen affirm that the Spirit eternally proceeded, or was eternally coming from the Father! This is the whole thread on which this *"doctrine"* hangs. I only instance this and cannot now pause on the others.

But besides this species of sophistry there is another more dangerous, because more specious. This is really as foreign and as barbarous a dialect as that we have noticed, though in Bible terms. It consists in selecting Bible terms and sentences and in applying to them ideas totally different from those attached to them by the Holy Spirit. Of this sort are the following: "The natural man, spiritual man; in the flesh, in the spirit; regeneration, washing of regeneration; ministration of the Spirit, demonstration of the Spirit; power of God, faith of the operation of God, the grace of God; the letter, the spirit; the old and new covenant; word of God; the ministry of the word; truth of the gospel; mystery, election, charity, heretic, heresy, blasphemy, church communion, baptism, faith," etc. The former dialect rejects the words of the Holy Spirit, and adopts others as more intelligible, less ambiguous, and better adapted to preserve a pure church. The latter dialect takes the terms and sentences of the Spirit and makes them convey ideas diverse from those communicated by the Spirit. We shall in this, as in the former dialect, specify one instance. Take for this purpose the sentence, *"Through faith of the operation of God."* This the populars use to designate a faith wrought in the human heart by the operation of the great power of God. But the Spirit of God intended by this phrase to show that Christians in baptism had represented to them their *resurrection* with Christ to a new life, *through a belief of the great power of God,* exhibited in raising Christ from the dead. So the wisest teachers, and so all the learned translators of the last century understood it, amongst whom are, Pierce, Tompson, Macknight, *et alios.*[11] Macknight reads it thus: "Being buried with him in baptism, in which also ye have been raised with him through the belief of the strong working of God who raised him from the dead." Now in relation to these two dialects there is one easy and safe course. The first is to be totally abandoned as transubstantiation and purgatory are by Protestants, and the other is to be tried by the context or design of the writer.

We cannot at present be more particular; but of these terms and sentences we shall not be forgetful hereafter. It is enough at

---

[11] Or, "and others."

one time to suggest them to the consideration and examination of our readers.

The adoption and constant use of this barbarous dialect was the cause of making divisions and is still one existing cause of their continuance. This style furnishes much matter, and many a topic to the gloomy Doctors who delight in metaphysical subtleties and gains them much credit for their skill in mysteries, which they exhibit in their weekly attempts to unravel the webs which themselves and their worthy predecessors have woven. Let it be remembered that, as these terms were not to be heard in the primitive church, in restoring *the ancient order of things* they must be sent home to the regions of darkness whence they arose.

Chapter Five

The Order of Worship[12]

We shall now inquire what was the ancient order of worship in the Christian church. Preparatory to this it may be expedient to consider whether there be any divinely authorized worship in the assembly of saints. As this is a theme of great importance, and of much difficulty with some, we shall bestow some attention to it. And in the first instance we shall attempt to demonstrate, from rational principles, that there is a divinely instituted worship for the assemblies of the disciples. In order to do this as convincingly as possible, and to circumscribe the arena of conjecture, we shall take but two positions, which we hope to hold as impregnable fortresses against all assault. These we shall exhibit in the form of dilemmas. The first is *Either there is a divinely authorized order of Christian worship in Christian assemblies, or there is not.* This every man must admit or cease to be a man. Now to remove all ambiguity from the terms *of* this dilemma, we shall explicitly state that, by a *Christian assembly,* we mean a congregation or assembly of disciples meeting in one place for social worship. The day agreed upon by Christians for this meeting is the *first* day of every week. The authority that ordains this day we have already noticed in this work, and it is not now a subject of inquiry. It is also unnecessary to our present purpose, inasmuch as this day is agreed upon by all Christians, with the exception of some Sabbatarians, for whose consideration we have something to say at another time. By the phrase, *"order of Christian worship,"* we do not mean the position of the bodies of the

---

[12] "A Restoration of the Ancient Order of Things — No. V," *Christian Baptist* Vol. 2, No. 12 (1825).

worshippers, nor the hour of the day in which certain things are to be done, nor whether one action shall be always performed first, another always second, and another always third, etc. Though in these there is an order which is comely, apposite, or congruous with the genius of the religion, and concerning which some things are said by the apostles; and, perhaps, even in some respects, these things may be determined with certainty as respects the practice of the first congregations of disciples; but that there are certain social acts of Christian worship, all of which are to be attended to in the Christian assembly, and each of which is essential to the perfection of the whole as every member of the human body is essential to the perfect man — is that which we wish to convey by the phrase, *"order of Christian worship."* These remarks may suffice in the meantime to prevent misapprehensions; but in the prosecution of our inquiries every ambiguity will be completely removed. We shall now repeat the first position we have taken — *Either there is a divinely authorized order of Christian worship in Christian assemblies, or there is not.*

On the supposition that *there is not,* then the following absurdities are inevitable: There can be no *disorder* in the Christian assembly, there can be no *error* in the acts of social worship; There can be no *innovation* in the department of observances; there can be no *transgression* of the laws of the King. For these reasons, viz. Where there is no order established there can be no disorder, for disorder is acting contrary to established order; where there is no standard there can be no error, for error is a departure or a wandering from a standard; where there is nothing fixed there can be no innovation, for to innovate is to introduce new things amongst those already fixed and established; and where there is no law there can be no transgression, for a transgression is a leaping over or a violating of legal restraints. Those, then, who contend that there is no divinely authorized order of Christian worship in Christian assemblies, do at the same time, and must inevitably maintain, that there is *no disorder, no error, no innovation, no transgression in the worship of the Christian church – no, nor ever can be*. This is reducing one side of the dilemma to what may be called a perfect absurdity.

But, to make this matter evident to children as well as men, we will carry it a little farther. One society of disciples meets on the first day morning and they all dance till evening, under the pretext that this is the happiest way of expressing their joy, and when they have danced themselves down they go home. Now in this there is no disorder, error, innovation, or transgression, for there is no divinely authorized order of Christian worship. The reader will observe that we do not suppose human laws or regulations of any consequence in this matter. Men may regulate the worship they require for themselves and for one another; and in relation to those regulations there may be disorder, error, innovation, and transgression. But as none but the Lord can prescribe or regulate the worship due unto himself and profitable to us; so, if he has done it, human regulations are as vain and useless as attempts to prevent the ebbing of the sea or the waxing and waning of the moon. But to proceed: Another society meets for worship, and they sing all day; another shouts all day; another runs as in a race all day; another lies prostrate on the ground all day; another reads all day; another hears one man speak all day; another sits silent all day; another waves palm branches all day; another cries in the forenoon and listens to the organ in the afternoon; and it is all equally right, lawful, orderly, and acceptable; for there is no divinely authorized order of Christian worship. We are then, on the principles of reason, constrained to abandon this side of the dilemma, and give up the hypothesis that there is no divinely authorized order of Christian worship. Now as one of the only two supposable cases must be abandoned, it follows by undeniable consequence, *that there is a divinely authorized order of Christian worship in Christian assemblies.*

Our second position we hope to make appear equally strong and unassailable. Having now proven that there is a divinely authorized order of Christian worship in Christian assemblies, our second dilemma is: *Either this Christian worship in Christian assemblies is uniformly the same, or* it *is not.* To clear this position of ambiguity, it will be observed that we speak of the assembling of the disciples on the day agreed upon for the purpose of social worship, and that the same acts of religious worship are to be performed on every first day in every assembly of disciples, or they are not. If the same acts of worship, or religious ordinances, or observances, be attended to in every assembling of the saints, then their worship is uniformly the same; but if not, then it is not uniformly the same. The position we again repeat, this exposition being given: *Either the Christian worship in Christian assemblies is uniformly the same, or it is not.*

We shall follow the same method of demonstration as in the preceding dilemma. We shall take the last of the only two supposable cases and try its merits. *It is not uniformly the same.* Then it is different. These differences are either limited or unlimited. If they are unlimited, then it is uniformly different; and what is uniformly different has no order, standard, or rule, and thus we are led to the same absurdities which followed from supposing there was no divinely authorized order of Christian worship, for a worship uniformly different is a worship without order. But supposing that those differences are limited, those limitations must be defined or pointed out somewhere. But they are not. Now differences that are nowhere limited or pointed out are unlimited, and consequently may be carried *ad infinitum,*[13] which is

---

[13] Or, "forever."

to say there is no order appointed, and thus we are again encompassed with the same absurdities.

To level this to every apprehension, it may be remarked that the worship of the Jews, though divinely authorized, was not uniformly the same. The worship at the feast of Tabernacles, at Pentecost, at the Passover, and in different seasons of the year, and even of the Moon, varied from what was attended to on ordinary occasions. These varieties and differences were pointed out in their standard of worship. But no such varieties are pointed out, no such differences are ordained in any part of the standard of Christian worship. Yet we find amongst the professed Christians as great variety existing as amongst the Jews — though with this difference, that divine authority ordained the one, and human authority the other. The worship of a class-meeting, of a camp-meeting, of a monthly concert, of an association, of a sacramental occasion, of a preparation, and of an "ordinary Sabbath," differ as much as the Jewish Passover, Pentecost, annual atonement, or daily sacrifice. Now there were in the Jewish state solid and substantial reasons for all these varieties, but in the Christian state there is no reason for any variety. The changing types of the Jew's religion have received their consummation, and now there exists at all times the same reasons for the same observances. There is no reason why a society of disciples should commemorate the death or resurrection of Jesus on one first day more than another. All the logic and philosophy of the age, as well as the New Testament, fails in producing the reason. He that invents or discovers it has discovered a new principle. But we are only establishing or demonstrating on rational principles that the worship of a Christian assembly is uniformly the same, and the method we have chosen is that of supposing the contrary and reducing the hypothesis to an absurdity, or a series of absurdities. In brief, the sum of our remarks on these positions is, that if the worship of the Christian church is not uniformly the same, then it is either occasionally or uniformly different. If uniformly different, then there is no established order, as proved in the first dilemma; and if occasionally different, there must be some reason for these varieties; but no reason exists, therefore a difference without reason is irrational and absurd. It follows then that there is a divinely authorized order of Christian worship in Christian assemblies, and that this worship is uniformly the same, which was to be demonstrated on principles of reason.

These positions are capable of rational demonstration on other grounds than those adopted; but this plan was preferred because it was the shortest, and, as we supposed, the most convincing.

This is only preparative or introductory to the essays which are to follow upon the ancient worship of the Christian church. We are hastening through the outlines and shall fill up the interior after we have given an essay on each of the following topics. They continued steadfastly in the apostles' doctrine — in breaking of bread — in fellowship — in prayers — praising God. As we have paid more attention in the general to the apostles' doctrine than to the other items, our next essays will be on the breaking of bread, the fellowship, and prayers of the primitive church.

Chapter Six

The Breaking of Bread (No. I) [14]

In our last number we demonstrated from rational principles, that there necessarily must be, and most certainly is, a divinely instituted worship for Christian assemblies; and that this worship is uniformly the same in all meetings of the disciples on the first day of the week: That *the breaking of bread* in commemoration of the sacrifice of Christ, is a part or an act of Christian worship, is generally admitted by professors of Christianity. Romanists and Protestants of almost every name agree in this. The Society of Friends form the chief, if not the only exception in Christendom, to this general acknowledgment. Their religion is all *spiritual* and may be suitable to beings of some higher order than the natural descendants of Adam and Eve; but it is too contemplative, too metaphysical, too sublime, for flesh and blood. We have tongues and lips wherewith men have been impiously cursed, but with which God should be blessed. We have bodies too which have become the instruments of unrighteousness, but which should be employed as instruments of righteousness. And so long as the *five* senses are the *five* avenues to the human understanding, and the medium of all Divine communication to the spirit of man, so long will it be necessary to use them in the cultivation and exhibition of piety and humanity. But we have a few words for them in due time, for we esteem them highly on many accounts. But in the meantime, we speak to those who acknowledge *the breaking of bread* to be a divine institution, and

---

[14] "A Restoration of the Ancient Order of Things — No. VI," *Christian Baptist* Vol. 3, No. 1 (1825).

a part of Christian worship in Christian assemblies, to be continued not only till the Lord came and destroyed Jerusalem and the temple, but to be continued until he shall come to judge the world.

That the primitive disciples did, in all their meetings on the first day of the week attend on the breaking of bread as an essential part of the worship due their Lord, we are fully persuaded, and hope to make satisfactorily evident to every candid Christian. Indeed, this is already proved from what has been said in the fifth number under this head.[15] For, if there be a divinely instituted worship for Christians in their meetings on the first day of the week, as has been proved; if this order, or these acts of worship, are uniformly the same, as has been shewn; and if *the breaking of bread* be an act of Christian worship, as is admitted by those we address — then it is fairly manifest that the disciples are *to break bread* in all their meetings for worship. This we submit as the first, but not the strongest argument in support of our position. We confess, however, that we cannot see any way of eluding its logical and legitimate force, though we are aware it is not so well adapted to every understanding as those which are to follow. Our second argument will be drawn from the nature, import, and design of the *breaking of bread.* This we shall first illustrate a little.

While Romanists, Episcopalians, Presbyterians of every grade, Independents, Methodists, Baptist, etc. acknowledge the *breaking of bread* to be a divine institution, an act of religious worship in Christian assemblies, they all differ in their views of the import of the institution, the manner and times in which it is to be observed, and in the appendages thereunto belonging. In one idea they all agree that it is an *extraordinary* and not an ordinary act of Christian worship; and, consequently, does not belong to the ordinary worship of the Christian church. For this opinion

---

[15] See Chapter Five, "The Order of Worship."

they have *custom* and tradition to show, but not one argument, worthy of a moment's reflection, not even one text to adduce as a confirmation of their practice. Who ever heard a text adduced to prove a monthly, a quarterly, a semi-annual, or an annual breaking of bread. This course regarding this institution, I conjecture, drove the founders of the Quaker system into the practice of *never* breaking bread — just as the views of the clergy make and confirm Deists.

Much darkness and superstition are found in the minds, and exhibited in the practice of the devout annual, semi-annual, and quarterly observers of the breaking of bread. They generally make a Jewish Passover of it. Some of them, indeed, make a Mount Sinai convocation of it. With all the bitterness of sorrow, and gloominess of superstition, they convert it into a religious penance, accompanied with a morose piety and an awful affliction of soul and body, expressed in fastings, long prayers, and sad countenances on sundry days of humiliation, fasting, and preparation. And the only joy exhibited on the occasion, is, that it is all over; for which some of them appoint a day of thanksgiving. They rejoice that they have approached the very base of Mount Sinai unhurt by stone or dart. In the opposite degrees of their ascent to, and descent from this preternatural solemnity, their piety is equal. In other words, they are as pious one week or ten weeks after, as they were one week or ten weeks before. If there be any thing fitly called superstition in this day and country, this preeminently deserves the name. A volume would be by far too small to exhibit all the abuses of this sacred institution in the present age.

The intelligent Christian views it quite in another light. It is to him as sacred and solemn as prayer to God, and as joyful as the hope of immortality and eternal life. His hope before God, springing from the death of his Son, is gratefully exhibited, and expressed by him in the observance of this institution. While he participates of the symbolic loaf, he shows his faith in, and his life upon, *the Bread of Life*. While he tastes the emblematic cup, he remembers the new covenant confirmed by the blood of the Lord. With sacred joy and blissful hope, he hears the Savior say, "This is my body broken — this my blood shed *for you*." When he reaches forth those lively emblems of his Savior's love to his Christian brethren, the philanthropy of God fills his heart, and excites correspondent feelings to those sharing with him the salvation of the Lord. Here he knows no man after the flesh. Ties that spring from eternal love, revealed in blood and addressed to his senses in symbols adapted to the whole man, draw forth all that is within him of complacent affection and feeling to those joint heirs. with him of the grace of eternal life. While it represents to him all the salvation of the Lord, it is the strength of his faith, the joy of his hope, and the life of his love. It cherishes the peace of God, and inscribes the image of God upon his heart, and leaves not out of view the revival of his body from the dust of death, and its glorious transformation to the likeness of the Son of God.

It is an institution full of wisdom and goodness, every way adapted to the Christian mind. As bread and wine to the body, so it strengthens his faith and cheers his heart with the love of God. It is a religious feast; a feast of joy and gladness; the happiest occasion, and the sweetest antepast on earth of the society and entertainment of heaven, that mortals meet with on their way to the true Canaan. If such be its nature and import, and such its design, say, ye saints, whether this act of Christian worship would be a privilege, or a pain, in all your meetings for edification and worship. If it be any proof of the kindness of the Savior to institute it at all, would it not be a greater proof to allow the saints in all their meetings to have this token of his love set before them, and they called to partake? If it were goodness and grace on his part to allow you twice a year in your meetings the privilege, would it not be inexpressibly greater goodness and grace to allow you the feast in all your meetings. But reverse the case, and convert it into an awful and grievous penance, and then grace is exhibited in not enforcing it but seldom. On this view of it, if it be an act of favor to command it only twice a-year, it would be a greater good to command it but twice or once during life. Just, then, as we understand its nature and design, will its frequency appear a favor or a frown.

It is acknowledged to be a blissful privilege, and this acknowledgment, whether sincere or feigned, accords with fact. It was the design of the Savior that his disciples should not be deprived of this joyful festival when they meet in one place to worship God. It will appear (if it does not already) to the candid reader of these numbers, that the New Testament teaches that *every time* they met in honor of the resurrection of the *Prince of Life,* or, when they *assembled in one place,* it was a principal part of their entertainment, in his liberal house, to eat and drink with him. He keeps no dry lodging for the saints — no empty house for his friends. HE NEVER BADE HIS HOUSE ASSEMBLE BUT TO EAT AND DRINK WITH HIM. His generous and philanthropic heart never sent his disciples hungry away. He did not assemble them to weep, and wail, and starve with him. No — he commands them to rejoice always, and bids them eat and drink abundantly.

Man is a social animal. As the thirsty hind pants for the brooks of water, no man pants for society congenial to his mind. He feels a relish for the social hearth and the social table because the feast of sentimental and congenial minds is the feast of reason. Man, alone and solitary, is but half blessed in any circumstances. Alone and solitary, he is like the owl in the desert, and pelican in the wilderness. The social feast is the native offspring of social minds. Savage or civilized, man has his social fire, and his social board. And shall the Christian house and family be always the poorest and the emptiest under heaven? Is the Lord of Christians a churl? Is he sordidly selfish? Is he parsimoniously poor and niggardly? Tell it not amongst the admirers of anniversaries! publish it not amongst the frequenters of any human association! lest the votaries of Ceres rejoice! lest the sons of Bacchus triumph!

The Christian is a *man*. He has the feelings of a man. He has a taste for society; but it is the society of kindred minds. The religion of Jesus Christ is a religion for *men*; for rational, for social, for grateful beings. It has its feasts, and its joys, and its ecstasies too. The Lord's house is his banqueting place, and the Lord's Day is his weekly festival.

But a sacrament, an annual sacrament, or a quarterly sacrament, is like the oath of a Roman soldier, from which it derives its name, often taken with reluctance, and kept with bad faith. It is as sad as a funeral parade. The knell of the parish bell that summons the mourners to the house of sorrow, and the tocsin that awakes the recollection of a sacramental morn, are heard with equal dismay and aversion. The more seldom they occur, the better. We speak of them as they appear to be, and if they are not what they appear to be, they are mere exhibitions of hypocrisy and deceit, and serve no other purpose than as they create a market for silks and calicoes, and an occasion for the display of beauty and fashion.

Amongst the crowds of the thoughtless and superstitions that frequent them, it is reasonable to expect to find a few sincere and devout; but this will not justify their character, else the worshippers of saints and angels might be excused; for many of the sincere and devout say, *Amen!*

From the nature and design of the breaking of bread, we would argue its necessity and importance as a part of the entertainment of saints in the social worship of the Lord in their assemblies for his praise and their comfort. We cannot prosecute the subject farther at present. We have been preparing the way for opening the New Testament in our next number, to produce evidence, and authority of a higher order. In the meantime, let the Christian who apprehends the nature, meaning, and design of this institution, say whether it be *probable* that it is, or could be an *extraordinary* observance, and not an ordinary part of Christian worship in the meeting of saints.

The Breaking of Bread (No. II) [16]

The apostles were commanded by the Lord to teach the disciples to observe all things he had commanded them. Now we believe them to have been faithful to their master, and consequently gave them to know his will. Whatever the disciples practiced in their meetings with the approbation of the apostles, is equivalent to an apostolic command to us to do the same. To suppose the contrary, is to make the half of the New Testament of non-effect. For it does not altogether consist of commands, but of approved precedents. Apostolic example is justly esteemed of equal authority with an apostolic precept. Hence, say the Baptists, show us where Paul or any apostle sprinkled an infant, and we will not ask you for a command to go and do likewise. It is no derogation from the authority for observing the first day of the week, to admit that Christians are nowhere in this volume commanded to observe it. We are told that the disciples, with the countenance and presence of the apostles, met for worship on this day. And so long as we believe they were honest men, and

---

[16] "A Restoration of the Ancient Order of Things — No. VII," *Christian Baptist* Vol. 3, No. 2 (1825).

taught all that was commanded them, so long we must admit that the Lord commanded it to be so done. For if they allowed, and by their presence authorized, the disciples to meet religiously on the first day, without any authority from their King, there is no confidence to be placed in them in other matters. Then it follows that they instituted a system of will-worship and made themselves lords instead of servants. But the thought is inadmissible, consequently the order of worship they gave the churches was given them by their Lord, and their example is of the same force with a broad precept.

But we come directly to the ordinance of breaking bread, and to open the New Testament on this subject, we see that the Lord instituted bread and wine on a certain occasion, as emblematic of his body and of his blood, and as such, commanded his disciples to eat and drink them (Matt. 26:26). This was done without any injunction as to the time when, or the place where, this was to be afterwards observed. Thus, the four gospels, or the writings of Matthew, Mark, and John leave it. At this time the apostles were not fully instructed in the laws of his kingdom; and so, they continued till he ascended up to his Father and sent them the Holy Spirit. After Pentecost, and the accession gained that day, the apostles proceeded to organize a congregation of disciples, and to set them in the order which the Lord had commanded and taught them by his Spirit. The historian tells us minutely that, after they had baptized and received into their society 3,000 souls, they *continued steadfastly* in a certain order of worship and edification. Now this congregation was intended to be a model, and did actually become such to Judea, Samaria, and to the uttermost parts of the earth. The question then is, *what order of worship and of edification did the apostles give to the first congregation they organized?* This must be learned from the narrative of the historian who records what they did. We shall now hear his testimony, "Then they who had gladly received his word were baptized, and about three thousand souls were that day added unto them; and they continued steadfastly in the apostles' doctrine, and in the fellowship, and in breaking of bread, and in prayers" (Acts 2:41). Other things are recorded of this congregation distinct from those cited, such as their having a community of goods, and for this purpose selling their possessions of houses and lands. But these are as peculiar to them and as distinct from the instituted order of worship, as was the case of Ananias and his. wife Sapphira. Their being constantly in the Temple is also added as a peculiarity in their history. But it may be correctly inquired, how are we to distinguish between those things which are as peculiar to them as their vicinity to the Temple, and those things which were common to them with other Christian congregations? This must be determined by a comparison of the practice of other congregations as recorded by the same historian, or as found in the letters to the churches written by the apostles. From these we see that no other Christian congregation held a community of goods; no other sold their possessions as a necessary part of Christian religion; no others met constantly in the Temple. Indeed, Luke, from his manner of relating the order of worship and means of edification practiced by this congregation, evidently distinguishes what was essential from what was circumstantial. For after informing us in verses 41 and 42 of the distinct parts or acts of their social worship, he adds in a separate and detached paragraph the history of their peculiarities. "Now," adds he, "all they who believed were together and had all things in common, and they sold their possessions and goods," etc. This, too, is separated from the account of their social acts of worship by a statement of other circumstances such as the fear that fell upon every soul, and the many wonders and signs which were done by the apostles. From a minute attention to the method of the historian, and from an examination of the historical notices of other congregations, it is easy to distinguish between what was their order of worship and manner of edification from what was circumstantial. And, indeed, their whole example is binding on all Christians placed in circumstances similar to those in which they lived at that time. For though the selling of their possessions is mentioned as a part of the benevolent influences of the Christian religion clearly understood and cordially embraced, as a voluntary act suggested by the circumstances of the times and of their brethren; yet were a society of Christians absolutely so poor that they could live in no other way than by the selling of the possessions of some of the brethren, it would be an indispensable duty to do so, in imitation of him who, though he was rich, made himself poor, that the poor, through his impoverishing himself, might be made rich. But still it must be remarked that even in Jerusalem at this time the selling of houses and lands was a voluntary act of such disciples as were possessors of them, without any command from the apostles to do so. This is most apparent from the speech of Peter addressed to Ananias and his wife, who seem to have been actuated by a false ambition, or love of praise, in pretending to as high an exhibition of self-denial and brotherly love as some others. Their sin was not in not selling their property, nor was it in only contributing a part; but it was in lying, and pretending to give the whole, when only a part was communicated. That they were under no obligation from any law or command to sell their property, Peter avows in addressing them, and for the purpose too of inculpating them more and more: "While it remained," says he, "was it not *thine? It was still at thine own disposal.*" You might give or withhold without sin. But the lie proved their ruin. Thus, it is easy to discover what was essential to their worship and edification from what was circumstantial.

Their being baptized when they gladly received the word, was not a circumstance, neither was their continuing steadfastly in the apostles' doctrine, in fellowship, in breaking of bread, and in prayers. This the order of all the congregations gathered and organized by the apostles, shows. Regarding our present purpose, enough is said on this testimony when it is distinctly remarked and remembered that the first congregation organized after Pentecost by the apostles, now gifted with the Holy Spirit, CONTINUED AS STEADFASTLY IN BREAKING OF BREAD as in the apostles' doctrine, fellowship, or prayers. This is indisputably plain from the narrative, and it is all we want to adduce from it at present. It is bad logic to draw more from the premises than what is contained in them; and we can most scripturally and logically conclude from these premises, that the congregation of disciples in Jerusalem did as steadfastly, and as uniformly in their meetings, attend on the breaking of bread, as upon any other mean of edification or act of worship. It cannot, however, be shown from this passage how often that was, nor is it necessary for us to do so in this place. We shall find other evidences that will be express to this point. We dismiss this passage, in the meantime, by repeating that the first congregation organized by the apostles after the ascension of the King, did as steadfastly attend on the breaking of bread in their religious meetings, as upon any act of worship or means of edification.

We shall again hear Luke narrating the practice of the disciples at Troas, "And on the first day of the week, when the disciples assembled to break bread, Paul, being about to depart on the morrow, discoursed with them, and lengthened out his discourse till midnight" (Acts 20:7). From the manner in which this meeting of the disciples at Troas is mentioned by the historian, two things are very obvious: First, that it was an established custom or rule for the disciples to meet on the first day of the week. Second, that the primary object of their meeting was to break bread. They who object to breaking bread on *every* day of the week when the disciples are assembled, usually preface their objections by telling us that Luke does not say they broke bread *every* first day; and yet they contend against the Sabbatarians that they ought to observe *every* first day to the Lord in commemoration of his resurrection. The Sabbatarians raise the same objection to this passage when adduced by all professors of Christianity to authorize the weekly observance of the first day. They say that Luke does not tell us that they met for any religious purpose on *every* first day. How inconsistent, then, are they who make this sentence an express precedent for observing *every* first day when arguing against the Sabbatarians, and then turn round and tell us that it will not prove that they broke bread *every* first day! If it does not prove the one, it is most obvious it will not prove the other; for the weekly observance of this day, as a day of the meeting of the disciples, and the weekly breaking of bread in those meetings, stand or fall together. Hear it again: "And on the first day of the week, when the disciples assembled to break bread." Now all must confess, who regard the meaning of words, that the meeting of the disciples and the breaking of bread, as far as these words are concerned, are expressed in the same terms as respects the frequency. If the one were *fifty-two* times in a year, or only *once;* so was the other. If they met every first day, they break bread every first day; and if they did not break bread every first day, they did not meet every first day. But we argue from the style of Luke, or from his manner of narrating the fact, that they did both. If he had said that on *a* first day the disciples assembled to break bread, then I would admit that both the Sabbatarians and the semi-annual or septennial communicants might find some way of explaining this evidence away.

The definite article is, in the Greek and in the English tongue, prefixed to stated and fixed times, and its appearance here is not merely definitive of one day, but expressive of a stated or fixed day. This is so in all languages which have a definite article. Let us illustrate this by a very parallel and plain case. Suppose some

500 or 1,000 years hence the annual observance of the 4th of July should have ceased for several centuries, and that some person or persons devoted to the primitive institutions of this mighty republic, were desirous of seeing every fourth of July observed as did the fathers and founders of the republic during the hale and undegenerated days of primitive republican simplicity. Suppose that none of the records of the first century of this republic expressly stated that it was a regular and fixed custom for a certain class of citizens to pay a particular regard to *every* fourth day of July—but that a few incidental expressions in the biography of the leading men in the republic space of it as Luke has done of the meeting at Troas. How would it be managed? For instance, in the life of John Q. Adams it is written in 1823, "And on the fourth day of July, when the republicans at the city of Washington met to dine, John Q. Adams delivered an oration to them." Would not an American, a thousand years hence, in circumstances such as have been stated, find in these words *one* evidence that it was an established usage during the first century of this republic to regard the fourth day of July as aforesaid. He would tell his opponents to mark that it was not said that on *a* fourth day of July, as if it were a particular occurrence, but it was in the fixed meaning of the English language expressive of a fixed and stated day of peculiar observance. At all events he could not fail in convincing the most stupid that the primary intention of that meeting was *to dine.* Whatever might be the frequency or the intention of the dinner, it must be confessed from the words above cited, that they *met to dine.*

Another circumstance that must somewhat confound the Sabbatarians and the lawless observers of breaking of bread, may be easily gathered from Luke's narrative. Paul and his company arrived at Troas either on the evening of the first day, or on Monday morning at an early hour; for he departed on Monday morning, as we term it, at an early hour; and we are positively told that he tarried just seven days at Troas. Now had the disciples been Sabbatarians, or observed the seventh day as a Sabbath, and broke bread on it as the Sabbatarians do, they would not have deferred their meeting till the first day, and kept Paul and his company waiting, as he was evidently in a great haste at this time. But this tarrying *seven* days, and his early departure on Monday morning, corroborates the evidence adduced in proof that the first day of the week was the *fixed* and *stated* day for the disciples to meet for this purpose.

From Acts 2, then, we learn that *the breaking of bread* was a stated part of the worship of the disciples in their meetings; and from Acts 20 we learn that the first day of the week was the stated time for those meetings; and, above all, we ought to notice that the most prominent object of their meeting was to break bread. But this, we hope, will be made still more evident in our next.

The Breaking of Bread (No. III) [17]

We have proposed to make still farther apparent that the primary intention of the meeting of the disciples on the first day of the week, was to *break bread.* We concluded our last essay on this topic, "And on the first day of the week when the disciples assembled to break bread" (Acts 20:7). The design of this meeting, it is evident, was to break bread. But that this was the design of all their meetings for worship and edification, or that it was the *primary* object of the meetings of the disciples, is rendered very certain from Paul in 1 Corinthians 11. The apostle applauds and censures the church at Corinth with respect to their observance

---

[17] "A Restoration of the Ancient Order of Things — No. VIII," *Christian Baptist* Vol. 3, No. 3 (1825).

of the order he instituted among them. In the second verse he praises them for *retaining* the ordinances he delivered them, and in the conclusion of this chapter he censures them in strong terms for not keeping the ordinance of breaking bread as he delivered it to them. They retained in their meetings the ordinance but did abuse it. He specifies their abuses of it and denounces their practice as worthy of chastisement. But in doing this he incidentally informs us that it was for the purpose of *breaking bread* they assembled in one place. And the manner in which he does this is equivalent to an express *command* to assemble for the purpose. Indeed, there is no form of speech more determinate in its meaning or more energetic in its force than that which he uses, verse 20. It is precisely the same as the two following examples: A man assembles laborers in his vineyard to cultivate it. He goes out and finds them either idle or destroying his vines. He reproves and commands them to business by addressing them thus— "Men, ye did *not* assemble to cultivate my vineyard." By the use of this negative, he makes his command more imperative and their guilt more apparent. A teacher assembles his pupils to learn-he comes in and finds them idle or quarrelling. He addresses them thus— "Boys, ye did *not* assemble to learn." In this forcible style he declares the object of their meeting was to learn, and thus commands and reproves them in the same words. So Paul addresses the disciples in Corinth— "When ye assemble it is *not* to eat the Lord's supper;" or, (*Macknight,*) "But you're coming together into one place is *not* to eat the Lord's supper," plainly and forcibly intimating that this was the design of their meeting or assembling in one place, commanding them to order, and reproving them for disorder. Now it must be admitted that Paul's style in this passage is exactly similar to the two examples given, and that the examples given mean what we have said of their import; consequently, by the same rule, Paul reminds the Corinthians, and informs all who ever read the epistle, that when the disciples assembled, or came together into one place, it was primarily for the purpose of *breaking bread,* and in effect most positively commands the practice. To this it has been objected that verse 26 allows the liberty of dispensing with this ordinance as often as we please. In the improved translation of Macknight it reads thus: "Wherefore, as often as ye eat this bread and drink this cup, ye openly publish the death of the Lord till the time he come." Either these words, or those in the preceding verse, ("This *do,* as often as ye drink it, in remembrance of me,") are said to give us the liberty of determining when we may break bread. If so, then the Lord's supper is an anomaly in revelation. It is an ordinance may be kept once in seven months or seven years, just as we please; for, reader, remember "where there is no law there is no transgression." But this application of the words is absurd, and perfectly similar to the Papists' inference from these words; for they infer hence that "the cup may sometimes be omitted, and under this pretense have refused it altogether to the laity." And certainly, if the phrase, *"as often as ye drink it,"* means that it may be omitted when anyone pleases, it is good logic for the Papists to argue that it may be omitted altogether by the laity, provided the priests *please* to drink it.

But neither the design of the apostle nor his words in this passage have respect to the *frequency,* but to the *manner* of observing the institution. If this is evident, that interpretation falls to the ground; and that it is evident, requires only to ask the question, what was the apostle's design in these words? Most certainly it was to reprove the Corinthians, not for the frequency nor infrequency of their attending to it, but for the *manner* in which they did it. Now as this was the design, and as every writer or speaker's words are to be interpreted according to his design, we are constrained to admit that the apostle meant no more than that Christians should always, in observing this institution, observe it in the manner and for the reasons he assigns.

And last of all, on this passage, let it be remembered, that if the phrase, *"as oft as,"* gives us liberty to observe it seldom, it also gives us liberty to observe it every day if we please. And if it be a privilege, we are not straitened in the Lord, but in ourselves.

"But," say some, "it will become too common and lose its solemnity." Well, then, the more seldom the better. If we observe it only once in *twenty years,* it will be the more uncommon and solemn. And, on the same principle, the more seldom we pray the better. We shall pray with more solemnity if we pray once in twenty years!

But "It is too expensive." How? Wherein? Is not the "earth the Lord's and the fulness thereof?" It costs us nothing. It is the Lord's property. He gives us his goods that we may enjoy ourselves. We never saw or read of a church so poor that could not, without a sacrifice, furnish the Lord's table. To make one *"sacrament"* requires more than to furnish the Lord's table three months. I hate this objection most cordially. It is antichristian — it is mean — it is base.

"It is unfashionable." So, it is to speak truth, and fulfil contracts. So, it is to obey God rather than man. And if you love the *fashion,* be consistent — don't associate with the Nazarenes — hold up the skirts of the high priest and go to the temple. But all objections are as light as straws and as volatile as a feather.

To recapitulate the items adduced in favor of the ancient order of breaking bread, it was shewn, as we apprehend —

1. That there is a divinely instituted order of Christian worship in Christian assemblies.
2. That this order of worship is uniformly the same.
3. That the nature and design of the breaking of bread are such as to make it an essential part of Christian worship in Christian assemblies.
4. That the first church set in order in Jerusalem, continued as steadfastly in breaking of bread, as in any other act of social

worship or edification.

5. That the disciples statedly met on the first day of the week, primarily and emphatically for this purpose.

6. That the apostle declared it was the design or the primary object of the church to assemble in one place for this purpose, and so commanded it to the churches he had set in order.

7. That there is no law, rule, reason, or authority for the present manner of observing this institute quarterly, semi-annually, or at any other time than weekly.

8. We have considered some of the more prominent objections against the ancient practice and are ready to hear any new ones that can be offered. Upon the whole, it may be said that we have express precedent and an express command to assemble in one place on the first day of the week to break bread. We shall reserve other evidences and considerations until some objections are offered by any correspondent who complies with our conditions.

The Breaking of Bread (No. IV) [18]

I do not aim at prolixity, but at brevity, in discussing the various topics which are necessary to be introduced into this work. We are not desirous to show how much may be said on this or any other subject, but to show how little is necessary to establish the truth, and to say much in a few words. We shall not, then, dwell any longer on the scriptural authority for the weekly breaking of bread; but for the sake of those who are startled at what they call innovation, we shall adduce a few historical facts

---

[18] "A Restoration of the Ancient Order of Things — No. IX," *Christian Baptist* Vol. 3, No. 4 (1825).

and incidents. We lay no stress upon what is no better than the traditions of the church, or upon the testimony of those called the *primitive* fathers, in settling any part of Christian worship or Christian obedience. Yet, when the scriptures are explicit upon any topic which is lost sight of in modern times, it is both gratifying and useful to know how the practice has been laid aside and other customs been substituted in its room. There is, too, a corroborating influence in authentic history, which, while it does not authorize anything as of divine authority, it confirms the conviction of our duty in things divinely established, by observing how they were observed and how they were laid aside.

All antiquity concurs in evincing that for the *three* first centuries all the churches broke bread once a week. Pliny, in his Epistles, book 10th; Justin Martyn, in his Second Apology for the Christians; and Tertullian, De Ora. p. 135, testify that it was the universal practice in all the weekly assemblies of the brethren, after they had prayed and sang praises — "then bread and wine being brought to the *chief brother,* he taketh it and offereth praise and thanksgiving to the Father, in the name of the Son and the Holy Spirit. After prayer and thanksgiving, the whole assembly saith, *Amen.* When thanksgiving is ended by the *chief guide,* and the consent of the whole people, the *deacons* (as we call them) give to every. one present part of the bread and wine, over which thanks are given."

The weekly communion was preserved in the Greek church till the *seventh* century; and, by one of their canons, "such as neglected *three weeks* together were excommunicated." — Erskine's Dissertations, p. 271.

In the *fourth* century, when all things began to be changed by baptized Pagans, the practice began to decline. Some of the councils in the western part of the Roman empire, by their canons, strove to keep it up. The council held at Illiberis in Spain,

A.D. 324, decreed that "no offerings should be received from such as did not receive the Lord's Supper." — Council Illi. can. 28.

The council at Antioch, A.D. 341, decreed that "all who came to church, and heard the scriptures read, but afterwards joined not in prayer, and receiving the sacrament, should be cast out of the church till such time as they gave public proof of their repentance." — Coun. Ant. can. 2.

All these canons were unable to keep a carnal crowd of professors in a practice for which they had no spiritual taste; and, indeed, it was likely to get out of use altogether. To prevent this, the council of Agatha, in Languedoc, A.D. 506, decreed "that none should be esteemed good Christians who did not *communicate* at least *three* times a-year — at Christmas, Easter, and Whitsunday." — Coun. Agatha, canon 18. This soon became the standard of a good Christian, and it was judged presumptuous to commune oftener.

Things went on in this way for more than 600 years, until they got tired of even *three* communications in one year; and the infamous council of Lateran, which decreed auricular confession and transubstantiation, decreed that "an annual communion at Easter was sufficient." This association of the "sacrament" with Easter, and the mechanical devotion of the ignorant at this season, greatly contributed to the worship of the Host. — the Bingham's Ori. B. 15. C. 9. Thus, the breaking of bread in simplicity and godly sincerity once a-week, degenerated into a pompous sacrament once a year at Easter.

At the Reformation this subject was but slightly investigated by the reformers. Some of them, however, paid some attention to it. Even Calvin, in his Ins. lib: 4. chap. 17, 46, says, "And truly this custom, which enjoins communicating once a-year, is most *evident contrivance of the Devil,* by whose instrumentality soever it may have been determined."

And again, (Ins. lib. 6 chap. xviii. sec. 46,) he says, "It ought to have been far otherwise. *Every week,* at least, the table of the Lord should have been spread for Christian assemblies, and the promises declared, by which, in partaking of it, we might be spiritually fed."

Martin Chemnitz, Witsius, Calderwood, and others of the reformers and controversialists, concur with Calvin; and, indeed, almost every commentator on the New Testament, concurs with the Presbyterian Henry in these remarks on Acts 20:7. "In the primitive times it was the custom of many churches to receive the Lord's Supper every Lord's Day."

The Belgic reformed church, in 1581, appointed the supper to be received every other month. The reformed churches of France, after saying that they had been too remiss in observing the supper but four times a year, advise a *greater frequency.* The church of Scotland began with *four* sacraments in a year; but some of her ministers got up to *twelve* times. Thus, things stood till the close of the last century.

Since the commencement of the present century, many congregations in England, Scotland, Ireland, and some in the United States and Canada, both Independents and Baptists, have attended upon the supper every Lord's Day, and the practice is every day gaining ground.

These historical notices may be of some use to those who are ever and anon crying out *Innovation! Innovation!* But we advocate the principle and the practice on apostolic grounds alone, Blessed is that servant who, knowing his master's will, doeth it with expedition and delight.

Those who would wish to see an able refutation of the Presbyterian mode of observing the sacrament, and a defense of weekly communion, would do well to read Dr. John Mason's

Letters on Frequent Communion, who is himself a high-toned Presbyterian, and, consequently, his remarks will be more regarded by his brethren than mine.

Chapter Seven

The Fellowship [19]

H KOINONIA, *koinonia*, translated fellowship, communion, communication, contribution, and distribution, occurs frequently in the apostolic writings. King James' translators have rendered this word by all those terms. A few specimens shall be given. It is translated by them *fellowship*, "They continued steadfastly in *the fellowship*" (Acts 2:42). "The *fellowship* of his Son, Jesus Christ" (1 Cor. 1:9). "What *fellowship* hath light with darkness" (2 Cor. 6:14). "The right hand of *fellowship*" (Gal. 2:9). "The *fellowship* of his sufferings" (Phil. 3:10). "*Fellowship* with the Father*" (1 John 1:3). "The *fellowship* of the ministering to the saints" (2 Cor. 8:4).

They have sometimes translated it by the word *communion*. "The *communion* of his blood" (1 Cor. 10:16). "The *communion* of his body." "The *communion* of the Holy Spirit" (2 Cor. 13:14).

They have also used the term *communicate* or *communication*, "To *communicate*" (Heb. 13:16) or "Of the *communication* be not forgetful, for with such sacrifices God is well pleased."

Where it evidently means almsgiving in other places, they have chosen the term *distribution*, "For your liberal *distribution* unto them, and unto all" (2 Cor. 9:13).

They have also selected the term *contribution* as an appropriate translation, "For it hath pleased them of Macedonia and Achaia to make a certain *contribution* for the poor saints at Jerusalem" (Rom. 15:26).

---

[19] "A Restoration of the Ancient Order of Things – No. X," *Christian Baptist* Vol. 3, No. 6 (1826).

It is most evident, from the above specimens, that the term *koinonia* imports a joint *participation* in giving or receiving; and that a great deal depends on the selection of an English term, in any particular passage, to give a particular turn to the meaning of that passage. For instance, *"The right hand of contribution"* would be a very uncouth and unintelligible phrase. *"The contribution of the Holy Spirit,"* would not be "much better." Again, had they used the word *contribution* when the sense required it, it would have greatly aided the English reader. For example — Acts 2:42. "They continued steadfastly in the apostles' doctrine, in the breaking of bread, in the *contribution,* and in prayers," is quite as appropriate and intelligible, and there is no reason which would justify their rendering Rom. 15:26 as they have done, that would not equally justify their having rendered Acts 2:42 as we have done. In Romans 15, the context obliged them to select the word *contribution,* and this is the reason why they should have chosen the same term in Acts 2:42. The term fellowship is too vague in this passage, and, indeed, altogether improper; for the Jerusalem congregation had fellowship in breaking bread, and in prayers, as well as in contributing; and as the historian contradistinguishes the *koinonia* (or "fellowship," as they have it) from prayer and *breaking bread,* it is evident he did not simply mean either communion or fellowship as a distinct part of the Christian practice or of their social worship.

Thompson has chosen the word *community.* This, though better than the term *fellowship,* is too vague, and does not coincide with the context, for the community of goods which existed in this congregation is afterwards mentioned by the historian apart from what he has told us in verse 42—There can be no objection made to the term *contribution,* either as an appropriate meaning of the term *koinonia,* or as being suitable in this passage, which would require an elaborate refutation, and we shall, therefore,

78

unhesitatingly adopt it as though king James' translators had given it here as they have elsewhere.

As Christians, in their individual and social capacity, are frequently exhorted by the apostles to contribute to the wants of the poor, to distribute to the necessities of the saints: as the congregation at Jerusalem continued steadfastly in this institution; and as other congregations elsewhere were commended for these acceptable sacrifices, it is easy to see and feel that it is incumbent on all Christians as they have ability, and as circumstances require, to follow their example in this benevolent institution of him who became poor that the poor might be made rich by him.

That every Christian congregation should follow the examples of those which were set in order by the apostles, is, I trust, a proposition which few of those who love the founder of the Christian institution, will question. And that the apostles did give orders to the congregations in Galatia and to the Corinthians to make a weekly contribution for the poor saints, is a matter that cannot be disputed, see 1 Cor. 16:1. That the Christian congregations did then keep a treasury for those contributions, is, I conceive, evident from the original of 1 Cor. 16:1 which Macknight correctly renders in the following words: — "On the first day of every week let each of you lay somewhat by itself, according as he may have prospered, putting it into the treasury, that when I come there may be then no collections."

Some who profess to follow the institutions of Jesus Christ, as found in the New Testament, do not feel it incumbent on them to make a weekly contribution for the poor, and urge in their justification, among other excuses, the two following: First, "In these United States we have no poor;" and, in the second place, "It was only to some churches, and with a reference to some exigencies, that those injunctions were published." The Savior said, "The poor ye have always with you;" but it seems we have

79

lived to see the day when this is not true, in the bounds of the New World. "But," says another, "the *poor clergy* exact from us all we can contribute, and all the cents which our mourning bags every week collect, are lost in this vast abyss!" "*Two wrongs* will not make *one right!*"

That some churches, on some particular occasions, were peculiarly called upon to contribute every week for one definite object, is no doubt true, and that similar contingencies may require similar exertions now as formerly, is equally true. But still this does not say that it is only on such occasions that the charities of Christians must be kept awake, and that they may slumber at all other times. Nor does it prove that it is no part of the Christian religion to make constant provision for the poor. This would be to contradict the letter and spirit of almost all the New Testament. For, in truth, God never did institute a religion on earth that did not look with the kindest aspect towards the poor — which did not embrace, as its best good works, acts of humanity and compassion: In the day of judgment, the works particularized as of highest eminence, and most conspicuous virtue, are not, Ye have built meeting-houses — ye have founded colleges, and endowed professorships — ye have educated poor pious youths, and made them priests — ye gave your parsons good livings; but, Ye visited the sick, ye waited on the prisoner, ye fed the hungry, ye clothed the naked Christian.

But some excuse themselves by shewing their zeal for sound doctrine. "We," say they, "do not build colleges nor give fat livings to priests." No, indeed, you neither contribute to rich or poor; you do not give to things sacred, or profane; you communicate not to the things of God, nor the things of men. You keep all to yourselves. Your dear wives and children engross all your charities. Yes, indeed, you are sound in faith, and orthodox in opinion. But your good works are not registered in the book of God's remembrance, and there will be none of them *read* in the day of rewards.

But this is not my design. *The contribution,* the weekly contribution — the distribution to the poor saints, we contend is a part of the religion of Jesus Christ. Do not be startled at this use of the term *religion.* We have the authority of an apostle for it. James says, "Pure and undefiled religion in the presence of God, even the Father, is this — namely, to visit (and relieve) the orphans and widows in their afflictions, and to keep unspotted by the vices of the world." There is a *sacrifice* with which God is well pleased, even now, when victims bleed no more. James has told it here, and Paul reminded the Hebrew Christians of it. And when anyone undertakes to shew that our present circumstances forbid our attending to a weekly contribution for the poor, whether in the congregation or out of it, we shall undertake to shew that either we ourselves are proper objects of Christian charity, or we are placed in circumstances which deprive us of that reward mentioned in Matthew 25. And if there is need for private and individual acts of charity, there is more need for a systematic and social preparation for, and exhibition of, congregational contributions. But let it be remembered that it is always "accepted according to what a man hath, and not according to what he hath not."

Chapter Eight

Questions about Restoration [20]

TO THE EDITOR OF THE CHRISTIAN BAPTIST
W— County, Ind. December 12, 1825

Dear Sir,

A sincere desire to know the truth as it is in Christ, is the sole cause of these lines. I need not tell you that I am not a scholar — that these lines will manifest. Neither do I approve of the popular doctrines of the clergy, or even of such an order of men; but think it my duty to let you know that I belong to a church called "German Baptists," sometimes "Dunkards," whose government is the New Testament only. They are not the same in principle or faith with those of the old connection in Pennsylvania, Virginia, Maryland, and Ohio; but an order that took rise from them in Kentucky, by one *Teacher*, in Shelby County, about six years ago, amounting now to about two thousand, having about 24 teachers, and increasing fast. Our views of Christianity you have expressed in the *Christian Baptist*, Volume 2, and on the *grace of God*, Volume 2, No. 8 and 9; and in the whole second volume I do not see anything to divide us in sentiment, though I do not approve of some things in your first and third volumes. The Calvinists here generally anathematize the *Christian Baptist* because it condemns their metaphysical speculations. I read your debate with McCalla, and also the first and second part of the third column of the *Christian Baptist*, and find myself edified, my views

---

[20] "A Restoration of the Ancient Order of Things — No. XI," *Christian Baptist* Vol. 3, No. 8 (1826).

enlarged, and my faith strengthened; yet I was astonished, finding you so great an advocate for primitive Christianity, to hear you say that whatsoever the apostles commanded constituted the practice of the first Christians, and yet not notice the plain commandment of washing feet, and that of the kiss of charity; and to hear you say that the practice of the apostles constituted a law for us, and upon this ground contended for weekly communion, and yet not stating that the *night* was the time, yea, the only time, according to Christ's institution and the practice of the apostles to observe this ordinance. Though I am not convinced of the necessity of weekly communion, not seeing how it could be kept so often in our back country, owing to our scattered state of living from ten to fifteen miles apart; yet I think, that whenever it is observed, it should be done according to the primitive model. This much I have written for your own meditation, and now request you to write to me personally, and give me your views on *trine* immersion. You have plainly proven in your Debate that immersion was the only baptism the New Testament authorizes; but you have not stated whether trine or single immersion is the proper action of baptism. In your debate you state that trine immersion was practiced within two years of the lives of the apostles; and we know, according to Robinson's History, that it was the practice of the Christians in the time of Constantine, and yet is among the Greeks. From the commission to baptize (Matt. 28:19), I yet think it is the proper action of baptism, and think that it should not be performed transversely, but forwards, in the most humble manner of obedience (Rom. 6:5). I have written this to let you know my views; and now beg you, in the name of Christ, to inform a poor, illiterate man, who never has had the opportunity of receiving education, though he has always desired it) the whole truth with respect to this matter. I wish you to be concise and very particular, as I shall depend on what you write me; and every earthly advantage and popularity would I freely forego to follow the truth. I am sincerely your friend, etc.

J.H.

REPLY TO THE ABOVE

Dear Brother,

For such I recognize you, notwithstanding the varieties of opinion which you express on some topics, on which we might never agree. But if we should not, as not unity of opinion, but unity of faith, is the only true bond of Christian union, I will esteem and love you, as I do every man, of whatever name, who believes sincerely that Jesus is the Messiah, and hopes in his salvation. And as to the evidence of this belief and hope, I know of none more decisive than an unfeigned obedience, and willingness to submit to the authority of the Great King.

Your objection to the weekly breaking of bread, if I can call it an objection, equally bears against the meeting of disciples at all, for any purpose, on the first day. For if you will allow that if they meet at all, there is no difficulty insurmountable, in the way of attending to this, more than to any other institution of Jesus. As often as they can assemble for worship on that day, let them attend to all the worship, and means of edification, and comfort, which their gracious sovereign has appointed.

As to the time of the day or night when it should be observed we have no commandment. But we have authority to attend upon this institution at whatever time of the day or night we meet. The Lord's having instituted it a night, will not oblige us to observe it at night, more than his having first eaten the Passover should oblige us first to eat a paschal lamb, or to observe it in all the same circumstances. We are always to distinguish what is merely circumstantial in any institution, from the institution itself. The disciples at Troas came together upon the first day of the week to break bread; and the apostle Paul commanded the disciples at Corinth "to tarry one for another, to wait till all the expected guests had arrived," which shows that it occupied an *early* as well as an essential part of their worship. Any objection made to the hour of the day or night in which any Christian institution should be observed is predicated upon the doctrine of holy times, or sacred hours, which are Jewish and not Christian. Besides, it is bad logic to draw a general conclusion from any particular occurrence. We might as well argue that, because Paul immersed the jailor at the dead of night, every person should be immersed at the same hour, as that because the Lord instituted the supper the night in which he was betrayed, it should be always observed at night. Nay, the same sort of logic would oblige us to observe it only the last night in our lives, if we could ascertain it, and to have no more than a dozen of fellow participants. We should, on the same principle, be constrained, like the Sabbatarians, to reform our almanacs, and to decide whether it was instituted at 9:00 or 12:00 at night, etc. But apostolic precedent decides this point, and not inferential reasoning.

As to *the washing of the saints' feet,* there is no evidence that it was a religious ordinance, or an act of social worship. Yea, there is positive evidence that it was not. Paul, in his directions to Timothy, at Ephesus, tells him that certain widows were to be supported in certain circumstances by the church. These widows were members of the church; and, as such, must have been regular attendants on, and partakers of all its institutions.

Now, in describing the character of those widows which were to be supported by the congregation, Paul says, "If she has brought up children, if she has lodged strangers, if she has washed the saints' feet, if she has diligently followed every good work." Had the washing of the saints' feet been a religious, or what is called a church or social ordinance, it would have been impossible for her to have been in the congregation, and not to have joined in it. He might as well have said, if she have been baptized, if she have eaten the supper, as to have said, "If she have washed the saints' feet" had been a religious institution. But he ranks it not amongst social acts of worship, not amongst religious institutions, but amongst *good works.* When then, it is a *good work,* it ought to be performed, but never placed on a level with acts of religious worship. It is a good work when necessity calls for it; and, though a menial service, the Savior gave an example that no Christian should forget, of that condescending humility which, as Christians, we are bound, both from precept and example, to exhibit towards our brethren in all cases when called upon. Besides the design of it at the time he practiced it, is ascertained from a regard to the mistaken and aspiring views of the disciples respecting the nature of places of honor in his kingdom.

It was a good work, and still is a good work, more frequently in Asia than America. The soil, climate, and dress of the Asiatic more frequently called for it, than our circumstances require it. But we argue not from these circumstances — we use them as illustrations of the fact that Paul the Apostle has positively decided that it is not a religious institution, an act of religious worship, or an ordinance in the church, but simply a good work, and I have experienced it to be a good work, in my own person, more than once, even in these United States.

Much the same sort of evidence exists in proof that the *kiss of charity* is not a social or church ordinance. A great deal more, however, can be said in behalf if it, than of either of the preceding items. It is argued that it is *five* times positively commanded in the epistles written to the congregations, set in order by the apostles. From this I would conclude that it had not been established by the apostles as an act of religious or social worship in those societies, as a part of their usual and stated worship; for if it had, there could not have existed a reason for enjoining it so repeatedly as we find it enjoined. Hence, we do not find one commandment in all the epistles to the churches, respecting baptism, the Lord's Supper, or the Lord's Day: certain things are said of them, and in relation to them, as already established in the church, but no command to observe them. From the fact of the kiss of charity being so often mentioned, and from the circumstances of the congregations to which it is mentioned, I argue quite differently from many zealous and exemplary Christians.

Another argument in favor of it is deduced from that fact that these letters were written to the churches, and that consequently the things enjoined in them, were enjoined upon the disciples in their collective capacity. True in part only. For it is not a fact that the injunctions in those epistles all respected the brethren in their meetings only, but also their conduct in the world, in their families, and in all the various relations of life.

It is admitted that the usual method of salutation in the East was, and still is, by kissing the cheek or neck of a relative or friend. In some countries, in Europe, too, this custom is quite common; but the farther West or North we travel from Constantinople or Rome, the custom is less frequent. Shaking hands is one of the most usual methods of expressing friendship and love in Europe and America.

Christians are to love one another *as* brethren. This is the grand standard of their affection. Whatever way, then, I express love to my natural brother, I should express it to my Christian brother. If the custom of the country and those habits of expressing affection which it familiarizes to our minds, require me to salute my natural brother when I meet him, by a kiss on the lips, neck, or cheek, so let me salute my Christian brother. But if the right hand of friendship and love be the highest expression of love and affection for a natural brother, to salute a Christian brother otherwise is unnatural. For example — suppose that after an absence of seven years, I were introduced into a room where one of my natural brothers and one of my Christian brethren were assembled, and that I should kiss the latter and shake hands with the former; would not this diversity be unnatural and contrary to the generic precept, *"Love as brethren."* I contend, then, that neither the customs in dress, wearing the beard, or mode of salutation, is the meaning of the requirements, of the precepts, or examples of the apostles; but that the genius and spirit of their injunctions and examples, are, *in these things*, expressed by the customs and habits which our country and kindred adopt, and by means of which we express the spirit and temper which they inculcated and exhibited.

But to make this a regular and standing ordinance of Christian assemblies, appears to be entirely unauthorized by any hint, allusion, or command, in the apostolic writings. I speak neither from prejudice nor aversion to this custom. For my own part, I can cordially comply with either custom, having been born in a country where this mode of salutation was more common than in this; but to advocate or enjoin it as of apostolic authority, I cannot. When misunderstandings and alienations take place amongst brethren, and a reconciliation has been affected; when long absence has been succeeded by a joyful interview; or when about to separate for a long time, the highest expression of love and most affectionate salutations are naturally called for, which the customs of the country have made natural. And these become *holy* amongst Christian brethren on account of the high considerations which elicit them.

In a word, whatever promotes love amongst Christian brethren, whatever may increase their affection, or whatever expressions of it can best exhibit it to others, according to the customs and feelings of the people amongst whom we live, is certainly inculcated by the apostles. And if Christian societies should exactly and literally imitate and obey this injunction, no man, as far as I can learn, has a right to condemn or censure them. Nor have they who practice according to the letter, a right to insist upon others to think or practice in a similar way, so long as they exhibit that they love one another as brethren.

With regard to trine immersion, and the manner in which the action should be performed, we have neither precept nor precedent. In the Debate alluded to, instead of *two*, it is, I think, in the errata, 200 years after the apostolic age, when we first read of trine immersion. That immersion is always spoken of as one act, is most evident from all that is said about Christian immersion. It is true that the scribes and elders, as indeed the Jews generally, had a plurality of *immersions*; but the Christian action is a unit. There is no command that a person should be immersed *three* times in order to constitute *one baptism* or immersion. Nor is there an example of the kind on record, not even a hint or allusion to such a custom. Therefore, we cannot teach it as of divine, but as of human authority. And in what position the body should be disposed of in the act, is as immaterial as in what fashion a coat or mantle should be made. To bring the Christian religion to inculcate matters of this sort, would be to convert the New Testament into a ritual like the book of Leviticus, and to make Christian obedience as low and servile as that of the weak and beggarly elements.

Thus, my dear sir, I have hinted at the topics you proposed. I should have written to you "personally" long since; but in such cases, where the matter is of general interest, I prefer, as opportunity serves, to lay it before the public. And as to the long delay, I have to urge, by way of apology, that I am this winter, more than ever before, absorbed in business of the highest, most solemn, and responsible nature. I have under my care the publication of a new translation of the New Testament. Though the translation was made ready to my hand, yet the necessary examination of every word, and comparison of it with the other translations of note, for the purpose of assisting the English reader with the best means of understanding this blessed book, has given me incomparably more labor than I had any idea of. It is, indeed, to me a delightful and profitable employment, having assembled all translations of note, and even those of no great reputation, I am under the happy necessity of reading, examining, and comparing all, and in notes critical and explanatory, elucidating the text when it can be improved. But a small portion of my labor can be seen, or will meet the public eye, because, in many instances, after the most diligent examination and comparison, the translation given is adopted in preference to all others; and my labor simply results in the conviction that the translation of the standard works is the best. It is a work too that I dare not delay, or yield to any other demands upon me, however imperious. I have more than 60 letters at this time on file unanswered, and many of my correspondents are got out of patience with me; but I have a good, or many good apologies to make. If they will only bear with me this once, I hope to make them returns in full.

Wishing you favor, mercy, and peace, from our Lord and Savior, and glad to hear from you at any time, I subscribe myself your brother in the hope of immortality.

A.C.
February 25, 1826

Chapter Nine

The Bishop's Office (No. I) [21]

A bishop without a charge or cure, is like a husband without a wife, a contradiction in sense, if not in terms. There must be sheep before there can be a shepherd, and there must be a congregation before there can be an overseer. There must be work to be done before there is occasion for a workman. From all which it is plain there must exist a congregation of disciples before there is an office, officer, call, ordination, or charge concerning them. A bishop without a congregation, a president without a people, a teacher without pupils, is like an eye without a head, a tongue without a mouth, a hand without a body. From these incontestable dictates of common sense, if there were not a hint in the Oracles of Heaven upon the subject, it would appear that the existence of bishops or overseers was, in the order of nature, in the order of reason, in the order of God, posterior to the existence of churches or congregations. But the apostolic writings are as plain as the dictates of common sense upon this subject. They teach us that the office of bishops was the last thing instituted, or, in other words, that the apostle and evangelists had fulfilled their commission (i.e. had proclaimed the gospel, made disciples, baptized them, convened them, and taught them the Christian doctrine) before they suggested to them the necessity, utility, and importance of the office of a bishop. Thus, we find the apostles in their subsequent or last visits to the congregations which they had planted, instituting, appointing, and giving directions concerning the bishop's office.

---

[21] "A Restoration of the Ancient Order of Things — No. XII," *Christian Baptist* Vol. 3, No. 9 (1826).

From these premises it must follow that, as the enlisting of soldiers is prior to their training; the making of disciples, to teaching them, the gathering of congregations, to setting them in order; necessarily the bishop's work is different from that of a missionary, a preacher, an evangelist, in the New Testament import of these terms. *That the work of a bishop is different from every other work requisite to forming a congregation is self-evident from one fact, namely,* THAT THIS WORK OR OFFICE DID NOT ORIGINATE UNTIL CONGREGATIONS EXISTED.

How congregations *first* came into existence, is one question; how they are to be brought into existence now, is another question and what is a Christian bishop, or his work, is a question essentially distinct from both. To arrive at clear and distinct views on any subject, we must simplify, not confound; we must take one topic at a time; we must view it in all its bearings, and still keep it separate and distinct from every other.

We are now on *the bishop's office,* as presented to us in the primitive congregations, and not the question *How these congregations were gathered then,* nor *How congregations are to be gathered now.* On these questions we have dropped some hints already and may hereafter be more diffuse. We begin with a congregation such as that in Antioch, or that in Ephesus. The apostles and evangelists had converted, baptized, and convened the disciples in those places, had opened to their minds the Christian doctrine. In process of time, they had so far progressed in this doctrine, as to be able to edify one another; some, as in all societies, progressed faster and farther than others. Some were better qualified to preside, to rule, and to teach, than others; and the constitution of man as an individual, and of men in society, is such as to require, for the sake of intelligence, order, peace, harmony, and general good, that there be persons set apart or appointed to certain functions, which are necessary to the good of the whole associate body. The exigencies of the congregations required this, both with regard to themselves and to others. Thus originated the bishop's office.

The nature of the bishop's office may be learnt either from the exigencies of the congregations, or from the qualifications by which the apostles have designated bishops. The qualifications which the bishop must possess show what was expected from him. These qualifications are of two sorts, such as respect the work to be done by the bishop; and, secondly, such as respect the dignity of character which his prominence in the Christian congregation behooves him to possess. The former are those which some call gifts, or talents, of the intellectual order; the latter are endowments purely moral or religious. Those with which we are at present concerned are of the intellectual order. These are comprised under two general heads, namely, *teaching* and *presiding.* He must be qualified to teach and be able by sound teaching both to convince and to exhort those who oppose the truth. He must *feed the flock* of God with all those provisions which their exigences require, or with which God has furnished them in the Christian institutions. He must *preside* well. He is from office the standing president of the congregation; and it being requisite that he should be one that presides well in his own household, plainly imports what is expected from him in the Christian congregation.

In our ordinary meetings, according to the prevailing order in our congregations, we have no need of a president — we only desire and need an orator. Hence, we have often been asked, *What are we to understand by a bishop's ruling or presiding well?* I have generally replied, (perhaps rather satirically,) that the ancient congregations were not so well bred as the modern; that they were apt to ask questions and propose difficulties; and some arose to address their brethren in the way of admonition and exhortation, but that we Americans were a well-bred people, had studied the etiquette of gentility in our meetings; and

95

that our bishops needed not the qualifications of a president of a family, tribe, or community, no more than the president of the United States wanted a lifeguard in these peaceful times, or a shepherd a staff to guard his sheep when wolves and dogs were extinct.

In what are called "meetings of business," once a month, or once a quarter, there is some apprehension that a president or "moderator" may be necessary, and the first thing done is to elect or appoint one; never considering or viewing the bishop as anymore president from office than any other member, a positive and explicit proof that even the *idea of presiding well is* not so much as attached to the bishop's office in these times, amongst the Baptists too.

A congregation of disciples, which is modeled upon the New Testament, will find that *presiding well,* is just as indispensable as *teaching well,* and that the prohibition of novitiates, or young inexperienced disciples, from the bishop's office, is as wise a provision as any other in the Christian institution.

The bishop of a Christian congregation will find much to do that never enters into the idea of a modern preacher or "minister." The duties he is to discharge to Christ's flock in the capacity of teacher and president, will engross much of his time and attention. Therefore, the idea of remuneration for his services was attached to the office from its first institution. This is indisputably plain, not only from the positive commands delivered to the congregations, but from the hints uttered with a reference to the office itself. Why should it be so much as hinted that the bishops were not to take the oversight of the flock *"for the sake of sordid gain,"* if no emolument or remuneration was attached to the office? The *abuses* of the principle have led many to oppose even the principle itself. We have said much against the *hireling system* and see no ground as yet to refrain; so long as the salvation of the gospel, the conversion of the world, and heaven itself, are articles of traffic, and in the market, like other commodities, accessible to the highest bidder. The motto over the spiritual warehouses is, *"The Highest Bidder shall be the Purchaser."* And we are persuaded by a hundred venal prints, that if the church had the bank of the United States, that of London, and Paris, it could, in twenty years, convert the whole world except for a few millions of reprobates. I say while such is the spirit breathed from the pulpit and from the press there exists ten thousand good reasons for lifting our voices like a trumpet, crying aloud, and sparing not.

But to discriminate on this subject, and to exhibit where, and when, the hireling's system begins; to graphically define, bound, and limit, beyond the power of cavil, on the one hand, and abuse on the other, has appeared to be a desideratum. While on the subject we shall make one effort here, subject to future and farther amendments, as circumstances may require.

A hireling is one who prepares himself for the office of a "preacher" or "minister," as a mechanic learns a trade, and who obtains a license from a congregation, convention, presbytery, pope, or diocesan bishop, as a preacher or minister, and agrees by the day or sermon, month, or year, for a stipulated reward. This definition requires explanation. That such, however, is a hireling, requires little demonstration. He learns the art and mystery of making a sermon, or a prayer, as a man learns the art of making a boot or a shoe. He intends to make his living in whole, or in part, by making sermons and prayers, and he sets himself up to the highest bidder. He agrees for so much a sermon, for fifty-two in the wholesale way, and for a certain sum he undertakes to furnish so many; but if a better offer is made him when his first contract is out, (and sometimes before it expires,) he will agree to accept a better price. Such a preacher or minister, by all the rules of grammar, logic, and arithmetic, is a hireling in the full sense of the word.

But there are other hirelings not so barefaced as these, who pretend to be inwardly moved by the Holy Spirit to become *ministers,* and who spurn at any other qualification than the *impressions* and *suggestions* of the Holy Spirit; who are under an awful *woe* if they do not preach; and yet agree *merely* in the capacity of supplies, or *preachers,* to act the preacher for some small consideration. Upon the whole, I do not think we will err very much in making it a general rule, that every man who receives money for *preaching the gospel,* or for *sermons,* by the day, month, or year, is a hireling in the language of truth and soberness — whether he preaches out of his saddlebags, or from the *immediate suggestions* of the Holy Spirit.

The Christian bishop pleads no inward call to the work, and never sets himself to learn it. The hireling does both. The Christian bishop is called by the brethren because he has the qualifications *already.* The minister says he is *inwardly called,* and prepares himself to be called, and induces others *to call him.* The former accepts of the office for the congregation of which he is a member, and takes the oversight of them, and receives from them such remuneration as his circumstances require; and as they are bound in duty to contribute to him, not for *preaching the gospel* at all, for this they have already believed, enjoyed, and professed; but for laboring among them in teaching and watching over them, in admonishing them, in presiding over them, in visiting them in all their afflictions, and in guarding them against seduction apostacy and everything that militates against their growth in knowledge faith hope and love and retaining their begun confidence unshaken to the end. The latter goes about looking for a flock, and when he finds one that suits his expectations, he takes the charge of it for a year or two, until he can suit himself better. The former considers himself the overseer or president of the *one congregation only* who called him to the office, and that when he leaves them, he resigns the office and is no longer president. The latter views himself as a bishop *all his life*. He was one before he got his present charge, and when he abandons it, he is one still. He has been called of God as Aaron was, and remaineth a priest forever. The Christian bishop was chosen and ordained from his outward and visible qualifications which the apostles described and required. The "minister" is licensed because of some *inward impressions* and *call* which he *announces;* or because he has been taught Latin, and Greek, and divinity, and because he can make a sermon, speech, or discourse, pleasing to the ears of a congregation or presbytery. Thus, they differ in their origin, call, ordination, and work. *Money* is either the alpha or the omega, or both, in the one system. The grace of God and the edification of the body of Christ, are the alpha and omega of the other. Money makes, induces, and constitutes the one, unites him and his charge, dissolves him and his charge, and re-unites him with another; again, dissolves the union, and again and again originates a new union. Hence in the hireling system there is a continual tinkling of money, writing of new contracts, giving new obligations, making new subscriptions, reading of new calls, *installing* of old bishops, and a system of endless dunning. In the other, the love of God, the grace of Jesus Christ, who gave himself for the church, the eternal ties of Christian affection, the superior blessedness of giving to receiving, of supplying our own wants, of laboring with our own hands when it would be oppressive to others, either to relieve us or others, the example of Jesus who made himself poor, are the darling topics and the constant themes. That the bishop who thus labors in the word and teaching is worthy of *double honor*, and *justly entitled* to the supply of his wants, whether of food, raiment, or money, or all. Paul himself declares, and reason itself teaches; and those Christians deserve not the name, who would suffer such a bishop to be in need of any necessary good thing which they had in their power to bestow. If he waves his *right* to receive it, he is the more worthy; but the right exists whether he uses or waves it; whether it is or is not recognized by others. So saith the Christian institution, so saith reason, and so say I. But of the bishop's office again.

The Bishop's Office (No. II) [22]

Some of the populars sneer at the term *bishop,* as if the Spirit of God had not chosen it tó designate the only legitimate "officer" in a Christian congregation, who is, from office, to teach and rule. They love *Rabbi, Rabbi,* or *Reverend* and *Right Reverend* too well to lay them aside, or to exchange these haughty titles for the apostolic and humble name of overseer or bishop. And I see that some of the Baptists too, who love the *present order* of things, and who contend for the traditions of the fathers in the mass, in their editorial labors either capitalize, or italicize, or by some outlandish mark, erect a monument of admiration at every inscribing of the name Bishop. Yet their *dear* "Confession of Faith" saith, p. 43 —

"8. A particular church gathered, and completely organized according to the mind of *Christ,* consists of officers and members; and the officers appointed by *Christ* to be chosen and set apart by the church, so called and gathered, for the peculiar administration of ordinances, and execution of power, or duty, which he entrusts them with, or calls them to, to be continued to the end of the world, are *bishops,* or elders, and deacons."

Some again, because of the impieties of England and Rome in appropriating this term to a man who wore a wig, and a gown, and trappings, have considered it very profane indeed, to call any man a bishop who does not wear a wig and kiss the pope's

---

[22] "A Restoration of the Ancient Order of Things — No. XIII," *Christian Baptist* Vol. 3, No. 11 (1826).

toe. But to those who have got an apostolic taste, the title or name of office which Paul and Peter adopted and designated is incomparably preferable to the prescriptions of Geneva or Westminster. I have lately heard that some Baptist teachers who at first recognized the "divine right," at least of the name, and were desirous of coming up to the ancient model in all things, are now startled, if not considerably shocked, when saluted "Bishop;" but the term *reverend* can be heard without any nervous spasm. Perhaps this may be accounted for on good principles; and, indeed, if so, it is the best argument we can find for giving an exclusive preference to the terms adopted and fixed by the Spirit of Revelation. The reason why they are startled at the title, on this hypothesis, they see some incongruity in its application to them. There is no incongruity arising from their want of an academical education, from their being merely acquainted with their mother tongue, from their not having a doctorate or an honorary degree. It is not on this account they are startled or affrighted at being called Bishop. But they never read in the New Testament of a bishop of two, three, or four congregations: of a bishop having the *"pastoral care"* of a church in Rome, and Corinth, and Ephesus—in Philadelphia Pergamos, and Thyatira, at the same time. They might have read of a plurality of bishops in one congregation, but never of a plurality of congregations under one bishop. This they may have read in the history of diocesan episcopacy, but not in the history of primitive episcopacy. But some of them are startled, perhaps, on another consideration. They were not made bishops according to law. Their declaration of a *special call* to some work entirely distinct from the bishop's work, was the ladder which reached from the floor to the pulpit. And they do not read that any were made bishops in the hale and undegenerated days of the Christian kingdom, because of their having declared that they were inwardly moved by the Holy Spirit to take upon them the office of a bishop. In fine, there is no occasion for being particular or minute in finding out incongruities, which may appear to some a good and lawful reason why *they* should not be so designated. But they can discover no incongruity in being called minister, preacher, or divine; for every one that makes public speeches or harangues on religion, is so called by their contemporaries. The term *reverend*, too, is become such common property, that the preacher of the dreams of Swedenborg, or the leader of the dance of a Shaker meeting is fully entitled to all its honors and emoluments — equally heirs to its privileges in this world and that which is to come. That some half-dozen of Baptist preachers have become shy of the name bishop, for the reasons above specified, is, indeed, a good symptom in their case. It proves that their acquaintance with the ancient order of things is increasing, that they see a discrepancy between the ancient order, and the present — between themselves and the bishops instituted and appointed by the apostles.

As to our Presbyterian brethren, they make little or no pretensions to the name. They are wise enough to know that it is unsuitable to their character; but they would have some to think, that their *minister* and Paul's *bishop* are one and the same character.

Our Methodist friends have not quite forgotten the glory and majesty of the Lord Archbishop of York: — for even until this hour arch-episcopacy has some charms in their eyes. In other words, a few of this brotherhood still like the remains of diocesan episcopacy. They seem to admire it, even in its ruins. I believe, however, such is the progress of light amongst this zealous people, that few, if any of their leaders, consider there is a divine right for either their bishops or form of church government,

other than *"vox populi, vox Dei."*[23] Yet still their "church government" has too many heads, even when the horns are broken off.

The good old High church bishops are not within the sphere
of comparison. There is no point of contact; no one side of the
system that can be measured by any side of primitive episcopacy.

Our Baptist brethren began in the spirit, but ended in the
flesh, on their adopting a species of presbyterial independency — licensing of preachers, and then converting these preachers into elders, with the exclusive right of administering "sealing
ordinances," and creating or finishing an order of its own kind.

But the fact is, very generally, that few of the leaders of religious assemblies seem to know, or are able to decide, whether
they should be called evangelists, preachers, elders, bishops, or
ambassadors, but the term minister or divine seems to embrace
them all.

To many it seems but of little consequence to be tenacious of
the name. Why not then call all the leaders priests? Why not call
them astrologers, soothsayers, or oneirocritics, if the *name* be in-
different? Because, says one, those names are used to denote
quite different characters. For the same reason, therefore, let the
names which the apostles adopted be used in their own accepta-
tion, and let those things, persons, and offices which the apostles
said nothing about, be named or styled as the inventers please;
but call not bittersweet, nor sweet bitter. Let us not call the messenger of a congregation, an elder. Let us not call a preacher, a
bishop. Let us not call a bishop a divine, nor a deacon a ruling
elder. In a word, let us give to divine institutions divine names,
and to human institutions human names.

Were Christian societies to constitute Christian bishops, and
to designate them by their proper title or name of office, many

---

[23] Or, "the voice of the people is the voice of God."

important results would exhibit themselves, amongst which none of the least would be the levelling the haughty and supercilious pretensions of those who claim another office under this name and designate themselves as the only persons to be so viewed and denominated.

Another happy circumstance resulting from this course, would be the discountenancing and suppressing the pretensions and enthusiastic conceits of those who are imposing themselves upon society, under the pretense that they are specially called and sent by the Holy Spirit of God to preach. If they are *sent* to preach, let them go to preach — but *they can plead no right to officiate as bishops under the call to preach.* If they are *called* to go and preach the gospel to every creature, they dare not, of course, refuse to go; nor dare they assume a work in relation to which they are not called, and to which no man was ever otherwise called, than as the brethren, under the direction of the Holy Spirit, called him. For amongst all the qualifications by which Paul would have a bishop chosen — the *modern special call is not to be found* — I again repeat, that the adoption of the course divinely recommended, would, in due time, suppress the impositions practiced upon the unsuspicious by a class of raving, ranting, mountebanks, who are playing themselves off as a kind of little half inspired ones, who just give to the people what they pretend they have got from heaven; and say that so clear is their divine mission and call, that eternal woe, awaits them if they preach not the gospel.

The bishops of apostolic creation are sometimes called elders — because they were generally aged persons, and always amongst the oldest converts in the community in which they officiated. But the office is nowhere called *the elder's office.* There is nothing in the term *elder,* which can designate the nature of any office. But the term *bishop* implies a good and arduous work.

While on the term *elder,* it may be remarked, that there is no greater incongruity than to see a stripling or a young man from twenty to thirty, styled elder; and if the name does not suit his years, it is a very strong reason in favor of the conclusion that the office of a bishop does not.

Here I had intended to have called the reader's attention to the call and appointment of a bishop—but circumstances beyond my control, forbid an effort of this kind for the present.

The Bishop's Office (No. III) [24]

It is admitted by the apostle Paul that a person not invested with the office of a bishop may *desire* the office. "If a man earnestly seeketh the office of a bishop, he desireth an excellent work." He then proceeds to lay down the indispensable *moral* and *intellectual* qualifications which he must possess. In doing which he plainly supposes that one may *earnestly desire* this work who is not eligible to it. Experience, also a good teacher, teaches the same thing.

But having already glanced at the moral and intellectual endowments of a bishop in a previous number, we proceed to his call and appointment to office.

In the first place, then, the *call* is predicated upon the qualifications—without these he is not eligible; with them he is eligible. Consequently, a due estimate of his endowments must be formed by somebody; and most certainly not by himself, nor by those who belong not to the flock to be instructed and presided over. By whom then? Assuredly by those amongst whom he is to labor, and over whom he is to preside. His qualifications in

---

[24] "A Restoration of the Ancient Order of Things—No. XIV," *Christian Baptist* Vol. 4, No. 1 (1826).

the intellectual department must then be viewed in relation to the capacity and attainments of the flock; for a man may be fit to teach, and to preside over one flock, who would not be qualified to teach or preside over another. The flock then in calling or electing a person to this office will turn their attention to themselves as well as to the candidate. They will consider his intellectual attainments with a reference to their own and will conclude whether his aptitude to teach and his capacity to preside is of such a degree as will correspond to their circumstances. If so, he is apt to teach them, and eligible to preside over them. His election or call is from them and must be audibly, distinctly, and emphatically expressed. They are constituted the judges in this case. For no matter how eagerly, he may desire or seek the office, he can make no pretension to it from such consideration. He cannot make himself an overseer. This the flock must do.

On the mode or manner of expressing this call or election we have only to remark that the inspired writers use the term which the Greeks were wont to use in their elections of officers. The inference is, that in using or adopting the same term, they attached to it the current ideas, which were, that the person to be appointed should be publicly announced and that by the voice or stretched out hand of the members entitled to choose, he was to be elected. The *consent* of the people or their wish unequivocally expressed, was all that ever was, amongst Jews or Greeks, deemed *essential* to the *election* or appointment of any officer. Whether the hand should be stretched forward, or elevated; whether the electors sat or stood, or whether they spoke aloud, each one separately or with one consent arose and simply answered in the affirmative, the election was always good and valid; —provided always the desire of the people was clearly and fully expressed.

As to the act called ordination or inauguration, if ever there was such an act, peculiarly so called, it consisted in the imposition of the hands of the seniors or elders of the congregation. The apostles did express their concurrence with the people's choice by an act of this sort, and when congregations were fully set in order there was always a plurality of elders or a presbytery instituted in each congregation, who always did express their concurrence with the brethren's call by inducting the elected into office by the joint imposition of their hands. But this eldership was not a collection of elders from different congregations assembled; but those of one congregation. — The history of this institution stands thus, and would have continued thus but for the man of sin; — Everything essential to appointment, call, or ordination was vested in the minds of the brethren. Their desires, however expressed, gave the office to the candidate, however he was announced. The apostles so taught them. They, in the first instance, took a part, not in the call or appointment; but in the introduction and inauguration of the bishops elect. This was done in conformity to the Jewish custom of imposing their hands upon the head of the person or animal devoted. This being done, a plurality of bishops being thus introduced into any particular congregation when, either the death of one of the elderships, or the increased demands of the congregation required another, the brethren called or elected and the eldership expressed their concurrence, and the brethren's desire, by a formal sign expressive of the devotion of the person to the work. I say this is all that can be legitimately gathered from the volume, as to *the forms of investiture;* but as to the *right* of the brethren so to choose, and of the bishop, *on this choice* to officiate, there is the amplest evidence.

Here I would take the liberty to remark that in process of time, as corruption and defection progressed, it came to pass that what was, with the apostles, but the mere sign or mark expressive of their concurrence with the brethren's election and appointment, came by degrees to be considered as the ordination itself, independent of the brethren's voice — Now no instance can be found in the inspired writings, where the circumstances are detailed, of the call and appointment of any brother to any office, where the call and appointment is not distinctly represented as the act of the brethren, and in no case is an ordination or appointment made without them. But their call is what, in all cases, gives the right to officiate. This is the *essential* thing, and the other accompaniments are the *accidental* properties of this thing.

The analogy between such an appointment and that of a presiding officer in a free community is as exact as any other analogy. For example, what gives any man a *right to officiate* as a governor or a president in a free community — Is it not the call and appointment of the people composing the community. Whether is it the *voice* of *the people,* or *the form* of *inauguration* after the people have made the appointment, which constitutes the essential consideration in creating such officers? The application is easy.

The Grecian and Roman republics, the commonwealth of Israel in its primitive integrity, the republics of America, and the congregations of Christians in this one instance are essentially the same. In *their first origin the people did everything, both elect and ordain.* No republic ever sent to another republic for their officers to come and make ordinations for them. No kingdom or monarchical empire ever sent for a foreign king or potentate to come and make a king for them. No Christian congregation, in the age of primitive propriety, ever sent to another for their officers to come and ordain officers for them. The imposition of hands, when first instituted among the Jews, was practiced by the laity.

In process of time persons were set apart in every community under every form of government for the purpose of inaugurating those constitutionally made officers. It was so in the Jewish, it was so in the Grecian, the Roman and the American republics. It was so in the Christian, and it will be so again. With the history of the world, with the pages of Jewish and Christian history before me, I would contend that any congregation has a right to call, appoint, or ordain any person to any office laid down in the volume, and to do all the acts and deeds thereunto appertaining, without calling to their aid the assistance of any foreign deacon, bishop or officer.

Chapter Ten

Love Feasts [25]

That the Bible is precisely adapted to man as he is, and not as he was, or as he shall be in another state, is with me a favorite position; and one, as I conceive, of much consequence in any attempt to understand the Sacred Book. Next to it in plainness and importance is this — that the religion of Jesus Christ is predicated upon the whole man, his soul, body, and spirit. There is not a power, capacity, or attribute, which man possesses, whether animal, intellectual, or moral, which it does not lay hold of, which it does not address, control, or direct, in the pursuit of the most dignified and exalted objects. From the loftiest faculties of the mind, down to the appetites and passions purely animal, it loses sight of nothing. Hence, we may say of it as the Savior said of the Sabbath, *"It was made for man."*

It is a religion essentially social, and the reason of this is found in the nature of man — for he is a social being. The religion of Jesus Christ refines the social feelings and gives full scope to the exhibition of all that is social in man. No man can therefore either enjoy, or exhibit it to advantage, but in the midst of Christian society. Hence "love to the brethren," and all that springs from it, forms so conspicuous a part of the Christian religion.

A Christian congregation established upon the New Testament exhibits the most perfect society of which human imagination can conceive. Every perfection and advantage that belongs to society is a constituent of it. When we have put every faculty into the most active requisition; when we have aroused all our

---

[25] "A Restoration of the Ancient Order of Things — No. XV," *Christian Baptist* Vol. 4, No. 4 (1826).

powers to discover or to exhibit the nature, properties, excellencies, and benefits of the most finished, polished, and sentimental society, we have only been seeking after or exhibiting that peculiar character of society which the New Testament gives birth to, and to constitute which is its highest object, as respects the present world. Neither reason, nor even fancy itself, can project a single ornament, can point out a single perfection or benefit that belongs to society, which does not belong to, form a part of, that society of which we speak.

But I speak not of a degenerated state of a Christian society, such as those dead and misshapen things which intriguing kings and sycophantic priests have given birth to; but I speak of a Christian society in its pure and primitive state, such as that formed by the direction and under the guidance of the Holy Spirit. Many societies called "Christian" are the habitation of envy, pride, ambition, selfishness, a rendezvous of moping melancholy and religious superciliousness; a conjunction of ignorance and superstition; a combination of gloom and invincible moroseness. A great majority of Christian congregations assume an aspect more becoming an assembly of pharisees and monks than of Christians. A severe austerity, a rigid sanctimoniousness, an awful penitential silence characterizes their interviews. Their Sunday apparel seems to sympathize with an agonizing piety within, and every movement indicates that there is something in their religion at variance with their lives and their comfort. These are but little things; yet they are symptoms of a diseased constitution, and like an unnatural pulse, assure the physician that the vital functions are laboring under a morbid influence. There can be no doubt to those who drink deep into the spirit of the New Testament, but that the aspect of a society of primitive worshippers was essentially different from ours. The hope, and joy, and love, and confidence in God, which their views of Jesus inspired, animated their countenances and their deportment, and shone forth in their whole demeanor; as the ignorance, the doubts, and fears, and awful uncertainty, of a company of cloistered friars and nuns, designate their faces and gestures. It is not going too far to say, that an intelligent mind makes an intelligent countenance, and exhibits itself even in the ordinary movements of the outward man. It is much more evident that the whole aspect and demeanor of a congregation of worshippers is an index to their peculiar views and sentiments. Who, that is acquired with the views and sentiments of the individuals composing any congregation, does not see, or think he sees, in the outward man the character he has formed of the inward man. This I do not say as if it were my design to enjoin upon individuals or congregations to cultivate a system of appearances or movements, comporting with the sentiments, views, and feelings of others; but to lead them to reflect on the *causes* of these things, and to inquire after what that was, and what that is, which distinguishes us from the primitive disciples.

This leads me to remark that the primitive Christians had, amongst other things which we have not, a particular kind of feasts, called in the New Testament, *"feasts of charity,"* or rather *"love feasts."* This was not a practice for which they had to work themselves up, but it was a natural and unforced expression of the spirit which dwelt in them. A marriage supper is not more natural than a Christian love feast. There does not appear any precept enforcing or enjoying such feasts in any part of the apostolic writings. This would have been as inconsistent with the genius of the book, as for it to have given a commandment that Christians should eat and drink together. It was as much the genuine result of their religion, as verdure is the result of the genial influences of spring. When God sends the rain and causes the balmy zephyrs to breathe, it is unnecessary to issue a command to the seeds of plants to germinate and grow. Thus, it came to pass as soon as the Spirit of God was poured out on Pentecost and disciples multiplied, they not only attended upon the ordinances of social worship enjoined upon them by the apostles, such as *"the breaking of bread," "the fellowship," "the prayers," "the praises,"* etc., but they were led to meet in each other's houses, and to *"feast with gladness and singleness of heart."* This going from house to house and eating their food with gladness and singleness of heart, or as it is more correctly and beautifully rendered, "and breaking bread from house to house, they partook of their refreshment with joy and simplicity of heart, praising God," is just what is fitly called a feast of love, or *the love feasts* of the New Testament; because Christian Love bade the guests, brought them together, and was president of the table.

Feasts, either public or private, are usually denominated from the cause that institutes them. Now when a number of Christians are invited purely on Christians' considerations to meet either in a particular family, or at a public place of rendezvous, for the purpose of social eating and drinking, or feasting; this repast, whether given by one individual brother, or made by the contributions of all, is a *Christian love feast.* To these feasts was added the song: yes, the sacred, song of joy and gladness was a prominent part of the entertainment: for it is added, "they partook of their refreshment with joy and simplicity of heart, *praising* God." What more natural than these Christian feasts? Refined and elevated sociableness is the direct tendency of the Christian religion. The table and the fireside; the scenes of festivity, of social converse, and of social song, consecrated by Christian affection, become as joyful and cheering to Christian hearts, as ever was the altar of Hymen to the bridegroom and the bride—as ever was the marriage supper to the nuptial guests.

When any intruded into these love feasts, or were bid to the entertainment undeserving of it, these were "spots and blemishes" in those feasts of love and are so designated by the apostles. Hence it is inferred that none but those embraced in Christian love were wont to be invited to those entertainments; and that no social eating and drinking of a mixed character, where our relatives and neighbors are invited, irrespective of Christian considerations, can lawfully be called a *Christian love feast* in the primitive sense of these words. It also follows that whenever a company is called together, all of which are disciples of Christ, to eat and drink, and to be cheerful, such a feast is a Christian love feast, and forms no inconsiderable part of that system of means which is wisely adapted to enliven Christian affection and prepare men for the entertainments of heaven.

When the ancient order of things is restored, these feasts of love will be found as useful for the promotion of humility, benevolence, joy, and peace, as they were in those hale and undegenerated days of primitive simplicity. They will be found as necessary for the perfection of enjoyment in this earthly state, as any of the acts of social worship are to the edification of the Christian community in their weekly meetings. They are obviously distinguished from any of the acts of social worship ordained for the whole congregation on the day of life and immortality; but houses are not more necessary to shield us from the inclemency of the weather, than those festive occasions are to the consummation of the entertainments, and finished exhibition of the sociability of the Christian religion.

Chapter Eleven

The Restoration of the Christian Spirit [26]

Amongst all that has been said in this work on the ancient order of things, we do not at present recollect of having received any objections from any quarter against any one position laid down in any essay under this head. We have received numerous communications presenting objections to some articles in this work, but none that we remember of against any one item which we have said belonged to the ancient order of things. To what this is owing I presume not to say. One thing is obvious from the face of this work, that our correspondents are not backward *in* exhibiting their objections, nor are we very scrupulous about laying them before the public. This silence, then, on this grand chapter of this work *is* to be attributed either to a general conviction, or a patient investigation not yet finished, or to an entire apathy on the subject. We would rather ascribe it to either of the former two causes, than to the latter.

Before we proceed to any new items under this general head, we shall offer a few remarks on that spirit and temper of mind which was exhibited while the ancient order of things stood uncorrupted, and which it may be presumed must be possessed and exhibited in order to the restoration of that order.

One of the most infallible signs of true conversion which I know anything of—and one which the ancient converts generally exhibited—and one which Saul of Tarsus at the moment of his conversion so eminently displayed, is couched in these words—"LORD WHAT WILT THOU HAVE ME TO DO?" This

---

[26] "A Restoration of the Ancient Order of Things—No. XVI," *Christian Baptist* Vol. 4, No. 5 (1826).

unfeigned and vehement desire to know the will of the Lord in order to do it, is, in my humble opinion, the surest and most general and comprehensive sign, proof, and pledge of regeneration. The spirit and temperament of the ancient Christians inclined and drew them, as the laws of gravitation do all bodies to the center of the system, to a most devout conformity to all the institutes of the Prince of Life. They loved his will supremely. Neither fire nor water, famine nor sword, good fame or bad fame prevented them in their obedience. They took joyfully the spoiling of their goods and loved not their lives unto death rather than renounce their allegiance in any one point to him who died for them. His laws and institutions were all in all to them. No scribe, no rabbi, no Sanhedrim, no human tribunal, no popularity amongst their own people or foreigners, no reproach, no privation could induce them to treat his will with either coolness, indifference, or neglect. They reasoned thus: If Jesus died for us, we owe our lives to him. We are his, and not our own. His will shall be ours; his statutes shall be our choice. Our only concern shall be, *"Lord what thou have us to do?"*

Let the spirit, then, of the ancient Christians be restored, and we shall soon see their order of things clearly and fully exhibited. "If the eye be sound the whole body shall be full of light;" and if the heart be right, the practice will bear the test of examination. To have the ancient order of things restored in due *form* without the spirit or *power* of that order, would be mere mimicry, which we would rather, and we are assured the primitive saints themselves would rather, never see. The spirit of the present order of things is too much akin to the spirit of this world. It looks with a countenance beaming too much complacency on the pride and vanity, on the tinsel and show, on the equipage and style, on the avarice and ambition, on the guile and hypocrisy of this world. Its supreme petition is not "Lord what wilt thou have me to do?" but, "O ye sons of religious fashion! Ye leaders of religious taste! ye synods and councils! Ye creeds and systems! ye mitered heads and patented divines! And thou, O Mammon! Tell us plainly, tell us fully, what you would have us to do to gain your admiration, and, if possible too, to save our souls." This is not the spirit of all, of any creed, or of any party; but this appears the leading and triumphant spirit of the present order of things.

The spirit of the ancient order always looked up to the throne of Jesus, while that of the modern looks around on the smiles of ecclesiastic rulers. The spirit of the ancient derived its joys from the complacency of the Founder of the Faith, the spirit of the modern, from the approbation of the leaders of devotion. The apostles' doctrine was the food and support of the former, while creeds and commentaries are the nourishment of the latter. The praise of God animated that — the praise of men enlivens this.

May I tell a little of my religious experience, as this is much the fashion now? I will once at least, comply with the will of the religious populars. Well, then, I once loved the praise of men, and thought that it would be a great happiness could I so shape my course as to merit the praise of God and the approbation of men. I saw there was a kind of piety the people of fashion in the religious world admired, and I thought that a few small additions to it might make it pass current in both worlds. I set my heart to find it out. I saw but little difference in many sects as represented true piety, but a good deal as respected show and ceremony. I thought that which was most popular might upon the whole be the safest, as it would make sure of one point at all events and might gain the other too. For there was a John Newton in the church of King Harry and a George Campbell in that of St. Charles. I vacillated here for a time. If I joined the most fashionable and profitable society, and adopted the most *genteel* order of things, I did not know but that if I were an honest and faithful member, like some of those good Churchmen or Presbyterians, I might chance heaven as well as they, and at all events I would be sure of good entertainment on the road. Yet I felt not the attractions of the love of God; but soon as I was enabled to calculate the import of one question, namely, "What is a man profited if he should gain the whole world and lose his life?" and soon as I understood that it was *"a faithful* saying and worthy of *all acceptations.* that Jesus the Messiah came into the world to *save sinners,"* even *the chief of* sinners, I reasoned on different premises and came to different conclusions. If bought at so dear a rate, and purchased at such an immense price, I found all my faculties, and powers, and means and opportunities were claimed on principles at which no generous heart could demur. Had I a thousand tongues as eloquent as Gabriel's, and faculties of the most exalted character, 'twas all too little to tell his praise and to exhibit his excellencies to men.

The only question then was, *how* shall I do this, to the most advantage? In attempting to find an answer to this, I found that there was a way already laid down, which, if I was adopted and pursued, must lead soonest and safest to this point. It was all comprised in two sentences — Publish in word what he has done, and as his own institutions will reflect the greatest possible honor upon him in this world, let them be fairly exhibited and the end is gained. This claim of thought just led me to the question, "Lord what wilt thou have me to do?" Now, in attempting to find an answer from his oracles to this petition, I took it for granted that there was no new communication of his will to be expected, but that it must be sought after in the volume. When any act of devotion or item of religious practice presented itself to my view, of which I could learn nothing from Master's Last Will and Testament, I simply gave it up; and if I found anything there, not exhibited by my fellow Christians, I went into the practice of it, if it was the practice of an individual; and if it was a social act, I attempted to invite others to unite with me in it. Thus, I went on purging my views, and returning to his institutes until I became so speckled a bird that scarce one of any species would cordially consociate with me; but I gained ample remuneration in the pursuit, and got a use of my wings which I never before experienced. Thus, too I was led into a secret, which as I received freely, I communicate freely. It is this: There is an *ancient* and a *modern order* of things in the Lord's house. Now I am sure that if all my brethren had only the half of the religious experience I have upon this subject, they would be doubly in the spirit of this ancient order, and their progress would be geometrically proportioned to what it now is, My *friends* will forgive me for so much egotism — and *my enemies will find fault with me at any rate;* so that it is little matter, as respects them, what I say or *do.* In the meantime, however, I cannot conclude without again remarking, that if the spirit of the ancient Christians and of their individual and social conduct was more inquired after, and more cultivated, we should find but little trouble in understanding and displaying the ancient order of things.

Chapter Twelve

Purity of Speech [27]

If all Christians *"spake the same things"* they would doubtless be of the same mind. Yes, but, says the philosopher, if they were all of one mind, they would all speak the same things. Grant, then, that *speaking* the same things is the effect of *thinking* the same thing; and yet, perhaps it might be true that speaking the same things might, in its turn, be the cause of thinking the same things. For example, William and Mary thought the same things concerning John Calvin—they spake the same things concerning him to their children and their sons and daughters thought the same things of him. This is true in the general.

It is no uncommon thing in the natural world for an effect to be the cause of another effect, and the last effect to be similar to its cause. For example, there is a chain of seven links. A person with a hammer strikes the first link. The motion of the first link is the effect of the stroke of the hammer; but the motion of the first link becomes the cause of the motion of the second, because of the impulse it gives it; and the motion of the second becomes the cause of the motion of the third, and so on to the end of the chain. In each of these effects, so far as they become causes, there is something similar to the first cause. Now it is much more obvious that, in the world of mind or thought, this similarity exists to a much greater degree than in the world of matter. The reason is men cannot think but by words or signs. Words are but embodied thought, the external images, or representatives of ideas. And who is there that has paid any attention to what passes in

---

[27] "A Restoration of the Ancient Order of Things—No. XVII," *Christian Baptist* Vol. 4, No. 8 (1826).

his own mind, who has not perceived that he cannot think without something to think about, and that the something about which he thinketh must either assume a name, or some sort of image in his mind, before his rational faculties can operate upon it; and moreover, that his powers of thinking while employed exercise themselves in every effort, either by terms, names, or symbols, expressive of their own acts and the results of their own acts? Now, as men think by means of symbols or terms, and cannot think without them, it must be obvious that speaking the same things and hearing the same things, though it might be alleged as the effect of thinking the same things, is more likely to become the cause of thinking the same things than any natural or mechanical effect can become the cause of a similar effect. This much we say for the employment of the speculative reader; but for the practical mind it is enough to know that speaking the same things is both rationally and scripturally proposed as the most sure and certain means of thinking the same things. On this view of the matter, I would predicate something of great consequence to the religious world. Perhaps I might find something in it of more real importance to all Christians of every name, than all the fabled powers of the philosopher's stone, had they been real. Perhaps in this one view might be found the *only* practicable and alone-sufficient means of reconciling all the Christian world, and of destroying all party-ism and party feelings, with all their retinue and train of evils which have been more fatal to Christian light and liberty than were all the evils which fell upon human bodies from the opening of Pandora's box, to the animal enjoyments of this world. But how shall we speak the same things relating to the Christian religion? Never, indeed, while we add to, or subtract from the words which the Holy Spirit teacheth. Never, indeed, while we take those terms out of their scriptural connections, and either transpose them in place, or confound them with terms not in the book. If I am not greatly mistaken, (and I beg to be corrected if I am) the adding to, subtracting from, the transposition of, and mingling the terms of the Holy Spirit with those of human contrivance, is the only cause why all who love the same Savior are disunited. Now every human creed in Christendom, whether it be long or short, whether it be written or nuncupative, whether it be of "essentials or nonessentials," whether it be composed of five or fifty articles — either adds to, subtracts from, or transposes the words of inspiration, or mingles things of divine and human contrivance together. No such volume, no such articles can be *the form* or a form of sound words. Every creed is a new *mold* of doctrine, and into whatever mold metal is cast, when molded it must assume the size and impress thereof. Let silver be cast into a French, Spanish, English, or American mold of the same size, but differently constructed; and although it is all the same metal, and of equal size, each crown, whether French, English, or Spanish, assumes a different stamp. Now the apostle Paul uses this figure (see the new translation), "Ye have obeyed from the heart that mold (or, cast) of doctrine into which you were delivered" (Rom. 6:18). Now does not reason and experience teach us that if ten thousand pieces of coin were cast into the same mold they would bear the same impress We have but one apostolic *mold of doctrine* in the world, and all the sons of men cannot construct a mold of doctrine like it. A human conscience cast into the mold of the Episcopalian, Presbyterial, Methodist, or Baptist creed, and a human conscience cast into the apostolic mold, all bear a different stamp. The Episcopalian, Presbyterial, Methodist, Baptist, and Apostolic coin, not only wear a different date, but a different image and superscription. Martin Luther's head, John Calvin's head, John Wesley's head, John Gill's or Andrew Fuller's head is stamped upon each of them. Not only is the *Anno Domini* different, but the image or head is different on each. They may be all silver of equal purity for aught I know, till they are tried in the furnace; but they are not one, neither can they be in image, superscription, date, and other circumstances, and therefore cannot pass current in another country. Let them, however, be tried with fire, and melted down, and all cast into the apostolic mold, and they will come out with a new image and superscription and pass current through all the empire of that head which is stamped upon them. The figure, I think, is the best in the world, and illustrates the whole matter. I am indebted for it to the Apostle Paul. He gave me the hint, and I am grateful for it.

Some of our Baptist friends here in Kentucky have tackled round and thought of a new plan of making a mold to give no impress or stamp to the coin at all. They will have no image, superscription, or date upon it. They will have the coin to weigh so many grains or pennyweights, but without a stamp. A plan of this sort has been lately proposed by one of our good Doctors; but to the astonishment of all, the first coin that came out of this new mold was inscribed with the number *"six hundred three score and six."* Let him that hath understanding explain how this could be. But of this hereafter.

Let then, but one mold of doctrine be universally adopted, of standard weight, image, and super scription, and every Christian will be one in every *visible* respect; and then, and not till then, will the kingdom be *visibly* one. There will be *one king, Dei gratia*, on every crown; and that crown, if of genuine metal, will pass current through all the king's dominions. It is admitted there may be some pewter, or brass pieces whitewashed; but the former will soon grow dim, and the latter, when rubbed a little, will shew a baser metal.

I may be asked; how does this correspond with speaking the same thing? I will tell you; it is but a figure illustrative of the same thing. The same image and superscription engraved in the mold, answers to the same things spoken in the ear and conveyed to the mind. The same impression will as made upon the mind as upon the metal. And did we all speak the same things we would be as visibly one as all the pieces of coin which have been cast into the same mold. I again repeat, *that this unity never can be obtained while any other creed than the sacred writings is known or regarded.* And here I invoke all the advocates of human creeds in the world: —

Gentlemen, or Christians, whoever or whatever you be, I will consider your attempt to disprove this position a favor done to me and the Christian world. None of you have ever yet attempted to show how Christians can be united on your principles. You have showed often how they may be divided, and how each party may hold its own; but while you *pray* for the *visible unity* of the disciples, and advocate their visible disunity, we cannot understand you.

But to come to the illustration of how speaking the same things must necessarily issue in thinking the same things, or in the visible and real unity of all disciples on all those topics in which they ought to be united, I will select but one of the topics of capital importance on which there exists a diversity of sentiments. For example: *The relation existing between Jesus Christ and his Father.* This is one of those topics on which men have philosophized most exuberantly, and on which they have multiplied words and divisions more than on any other subject of human contemplation Hence have arisen the Trinitarian, Arian, Semi-Arian, Sabellian, Unitarian, and Socinian hypotheses. It is impossible that all these can be true, and yet it is possible that they all may be false theories Now each of these theories has given rise to diction, phraseology, and style of speaking peculiar to itself. They do not all speak the same things of the Father, Son, and Holy Spirit. But all who do speak the same things belong to one theory. Scripture words and sentences are quoted by each of the theorists, and to these words are added expositions and definitions which give a peculiar direction to the words of the Holy

Spirit. Some portions are considered by each theorist as peculiar favorable to his views, while others are not often quoted, and if quoted at all, are clogged with embarrassing explanations. Some of the words of the Holy Spirit are quoted with great pleasure and others with great reluctance. And why? Because the former are supposed more favorable to the theory than the latter. I have often seen with what pleasure the Arian dwells upon the words *"first born of every creature;" "the beginning of the creation of God."* And how seldom, and with what reluctance, he quotes *"I am Alpha and Omega, the First and the Last;"* "In the beginning was the word, and the word was with God, and the word was God." Again, the Socinian emphasizes with great force upon the words *"The man Christ Jesus;"* but never dwells with delight upon this sentence, "Who being in the form of God, did not think it robbery to be like God." The Trinitarian rejoices that "there are three that bear record in heaven, the Father, the Word, and the Spirit, and that these three are one;" that Jesus said, "I and my Father are one," etc. But seldom does he quote on this subject the texts on which the Arian and Socinian dwell with pleasure. Not one of them will quote with equal pleasure or readiness everything said on this subject; and had they the liberty they would trim and *improve* the apostles' style to suit their respective theories. They would do, as I heard a preacher do this week, quote the scriptures; thus, "if any come unto you and bring not the scriptures thus; "If any come unto you and bring not the doctrine of the absolute, unoriginated and infinite divinity, the doctrine of the eternal filiation and generation of Jesus Christ, receive him not into your house." They do not speak the same things of the Father, the Son, and the Holy Spirit. Now, suppose that all these would abandon every word and sentence not found in the Bible on this subject, and without explanation, limitation, or enlargement, quote with equal pleasure and readiness, and apply on every suitable occasion, every word and sentence found in the volume, to the Father, to the Son, and to the Holy Spirit; how long would divisions on this subject exist? *It would be impossible to perpetuate them on this plan.* I ask the world if it would not? But, says an objector, there would be as many opinions under any other phraseology as the present. This might be for the present generation, but they could not be perpetuated. And as to any injury a private opinion may do to the possessor, it could, on this principle, do none to society.

Again, could not men believe in, obey, love, fear, and rejoice in Jesus Christ as readily and to as great a degree by speaking and hearing all the words and sentences in the volume, as they now do in all the varieties of their new nomenclature. Let them then be cast into the same mold; that is, speak and hear the same things, and there would not be a Trinitarian, Arian, Semi-Arian, Unitarian, Socinian, or anything else but a Christian on this subject, or an infidel in the world. It would be so on all other topics as on that instance if the same principle were to be adopted.

Men would, on this principle, learn to appreciate and love one another, and to estimate human character on the real standard of piety and moral rectitude. Unfeigned obedience to the Lord, guileless benevolence to all men, and pure Christian affection to the household of faith, would be the principle of appreciation of human character. Not our wild reveries, our orthodox jargon, or our heterodox paradoxes would be of paramount importance. Never can this state be induced until a *pure speech* be restored — until the language of Canaan be spoken by all the seed of Abraham.

Our confessions of faith, our additions to, our subtractions from, our transpositions of, and our extractions out of the book of God, are all in open hostility to the restoration of a pure speech, and are all under the curse, and we are punished with famine and sterility on account of them. I have seen a confession of faith all in Bible terms, extracted and transposed, like putting the eyes and ears and tongue in the right hand. Now I object as much to a creed in Bible terms transposed and extracted, as I do to worshipping the Virgin Mary instead of Jesus the Messiah. The transposition of the terms or the extraction of sentences from their connections is just as pernicious as any human innovation. Samples of this sort will be afforded at another time.

No man is to *be debarred the Christian church who* does *not deny in word or in works the declarations of the Holy Spirit,* and no man is to be received into the Christian community because he expresses himself in a style or in terms not found in the Christian books; which must be the case when a person is obliged to express himself in the corrupt speech or in the appropriated style of a sectarian creed in order to his admission.

Chapter Thirteen

Advocates for the Present Order of Things [28]

The present general order of things is exhibited in miniature in the preceding remarks. There are many who advocate the present order of things — not, we hope, the effects of that order, but the system of things which legitimately issues in these results. They are, to say the least, false reasoners, or fallacious philosophers. They do not assign to effects their proper causes, or to causes their proper results. True philosophy consists in assigning effects to their true causes; false philosophy, in assigning effects to other causes than their own. We have often heard much of how the Lord has blessed the present order of things by the numerous converts and large accessions made to congregations under the reigning systems. This is most fallacious and dangerous logic. If it were true philosophy, it would equally prove that infant sprinkling, the invocation of saints, and the whole system of papistical and protestant managements were of divine origin and approbation. For how often do we hear the Papist and the Protestant appealing to the mighty achievements of their leaders in proof that the Lord is with them, and that he countenances all their movements? Each party numbers its Israel every year, and capitalizes its converts, in attestation that the Lord is there. Scarce a revival comes, but Presbyterians, Methodists, and Baptists come in for a share; though, in general, the two formers outcount the latter. Now if the Baptist annual converts prove that the present order of things is of divine origin amongst them, it will as logically prove that the present order of things amongst

---

[28] "A Restoration of the Ancient Order of Things — No. XVIII," *Christian Baptist* Vol. 4, No. 9 (1827).

Catholics, Presbyterians, and Protestants, is of divine approbation. All that my reasoning powers can conclude from these premises, is, *first,* that if the Lord's hand is not in these accessions, they are equally deceived; and though in different degrees, all distant from the equator of truth. One is ten degrees south; another, ten degrees north; and though twenty degrees apart, they are equally distant from the equator of true religion. But, in the *second* place, if the Lord's hand is in these accessions, then it proves that he disdains equally their systems and their order and bestows his favors indiscriminately on all. It cannot be argued that he approves all their systems; for this would terminate in the most absurd results. He would then approve of Papacy. Episcopacy, Presbytery, and Independency—of infant sprinkling and of believer's immersion, and of a hundred things flatly contradictory to each other. I say, then, it proves, on the best hypothesis, that he disdains all their systems and their order, and that he loudly proclaims it by the distributions of his favor upon the Baptist order, the Methodist order, the Presbyterian order, and so forth. If the Lord approved of one of the present systems, he would confer all his favors upon that people; or, in other words, he would assemble his elect under that standard, and signalize them as he once did the only nation he selected and made his own. They could exclaim, What people like us! What people hath the Lord blessed as he hath blessed us! I say, then, that to my reasoning faculties, the logic of the Baptist Recorder or that of the Presbyterian Luminary now confederated proves not that the Lord approbates that for which they contend, namely, the present order of things in their respective circles, but that he equally disdains both their orders. I would like to see them *try* their logic here. He sends his gospel to them all, on the supposition that the work of these revivals is his, and thereby calls them to reformation. I have no idea of magnifying molehills into mountains, nor of consecrating the language of

Ashdod into that of Canaan; I have no idea of amalgamating oil and water, of christening pagans, or of paganizing Christians; I have no idea of raising up a holy seed from Egyptian or Babylonish wives, nor of proving that the Lord approves the present order of things, because the Methodist and Baptists annually count twenty thousand converts a-piece.

During the ancient order of things there was no church meetings for the purpose of receiving candidates for immersion. There were no monthly meetings to decide who should be baptized. There was no person who held his membership in one church and had the pastoral care of another in which he was not a member, and to which he was not amenable, as is now the case very generally. There was no church in those days of primitive integrity, composed of a hundred members, which, in a case of discipline, gave only eleven votes, six against and five for the delinquent, and then excommunicated him. There was no deacon appointed solely for the purpose of carrying about a plate four times a year There was no society whose whole code of discipline was Matthew 18. There was no one who had any formulary, creed, or confession, other than the apostolic writings. Now let him that affirms to the contrary remember that the proof lies upon him. And we will assure him that his proof will be faithfully published by us, should he send it for that purpose. The subjects introduced here are intended for future development.

Chapter Fourteen

The Deacon's Office [29]

The time once was that every Christian congregation had a treasury. In those days they required a steward, a treasurer, or a deacon, or more than one, as the exigencies demanded. For although the terms *steward, treasurer, almoner,* and *deacon,* are not perfectly synonymous, they nevertheless express the office and duty of the scriptural deacon. The term *deacon,* as all know, is equivalent to the English word *servant.* But the word servant is a very general term, and in the state signifies every public officer, from the president down to the constable. They are all servants of the state. So the apostles, evangelists, prophets, and bishops were all servants of the Lord and of the church. But there was one set of servants in the apostolic churches who were emphatically the servants of the church in its temporal concerns. These were the deacons, or stewards, or treasurers of the church. For as the deacon's office had respect to the temporalities of the church, and as these are in general some way connected with pecuniary matters, the office of treasurer and almoner is identified with, or is the same as that of deacon; so much so that some translators have, out of regard more to the application than to the literal import of the term *diakonos,* uniformly translated it *almoner.*

The plain simple state of the case is this: Christian congregations, in primitive times, had need of money or earthly things, as well as we. They had rich and poor members. Their poor were such as could not, either through bodily infirmities, or through

---

[29] "A Restoration of the Ancient Order of Things — No. XIX," *Christian Baptist* Vol. 4, No. 10 (1827).

the inadequate proceeds of their labor in times of embarrassment, furnish their own tables. Those who had to spare were then called upon to supply their wants. And in many instances, they not only contribute to the wants of their own poor, but to the wants of those of remote Christian communities, in times of general scarcity or pecuniary difficulties. Contributions, generally called the *fellowship,* were statedly attended to in all their meetings. So, Paul gave directions to all the churches in Galatia and elsewhere to replenish the treasury every first day as the Lord had prospered them in their temporal avocations. A deacon or deacons had the charge of this treasury and were *ex-officio*[30] treasurers; but this was not all. They were not only to take care of the contributions, but to dispense or appropriate them according to the directions of the brethren. Thus, they were *stewards.* And as the poor were those in whose behalf this fund was created, and as the deacons dispensed to them, they became, *ex-officio, almoners* of the poor.

As they had in those days of primitive simplicity so many different sorts of funds and officers as we have in this age of complexity; the deacons attended to all pecuniary matters, and out of the same fund three sets of tables were furnished. These were the Lord's table, the bishop's table, and the poor's table. A plurality of deacons was in most instances necessary because of the attention required from them and the trust reposed in them. It was not so much per annum to the bishop, nor so much per annum to the poor, nor so much per annum to the Lord's table; but according to the exigencies of each and the ability to contribute, was the extent of the treasury and the distributions of the stewards or deacons of the congregation. In this state of things, the deacons had something to do. They were intimately acquainted with the families and wants of the brethren, and in paying a

---

[30] Or, "from the office."

Christian regard to these and the duties of their office they obtained an honorable rank and great boldness in the faith, or fluency in the doctrine of Christ. Conversant with the sick and the poor, intimate with the rich and more affluent brethren, familiar with all, and devoted to the Lord in all their services, they became eminent for their piety and charity, and of high reputation amongst their brethren. Once every week these contributions were made, and as often are the appropriations made in times and circumstances that required them. Out of the church's treasury, then, the poor and distressed widow above three score, or the sick and afflicted disciples was relieved. The Lord's table was continually furnished with bread and wine. The bishops' also, according to their labors and their need, were supplied. And thus, everything was promptly attended to in the Lord's institution which could afford spiritual and temporal comfort to all the subjects of his kingdom.

Amongst the Greeks who paid so much regard to differences of sex, female deacons, or deaconesses, were appointed to visit and wait upon the sisters. Of this sort was Phebe of Cenchrea, and other persons mentioned in the New Testament, who labored in the gospel. The seven persons mentioned and appointed to the service of tables (Acts 6), though not so denominated, were nevertheless invested with and fully possessed of this office. The treasury was entrusted to them — the widows' tables, and every table which required service was attended by them. The direction given to the Corinthians respecting the treasury, and the instructions to Timothy and Titus concerning the choice of deacons, also concerning the support of widows and bishops, all concur in furnishing the above views of this office and work. But how has it degenerated in modern times into a frivolous and unmeaning carrying about a plate once-a-quarter, in all the meagre pomp of a vain world — mere pompous etiquette, without use or meaning. Often, we find the office of

treasurer and deacon contradistinguished, as that of a moderator and bishop in the same congregation. It is a scriptural insult
to appoint a moderator where there is a bishop, and the same to
appoint a treasurer where there is a deacon. The deacon is *ex-
officio*, treasurer, and the bishop, *ex-officio*, moderator or president. To appoint a president in any meeting where there is an
appointed bishop, it is in effect saying that the bishop is not qualified to keep order; and to appoint a treasurer where there is a
deacon, it is in effect saying he is not to be trusted, or not qualified for his office. The office itself suggests the propriety of those
directions and qualifications laid down for both the deacons and
deaconesses in Paul's letters before mentioned. What a wise, benevolent, and independent institution, a Christian congregation
is! Nothing is left out of view which can contribute to the temporal and spiritual weal of the brotherhood. They meet in full
assembly once every week to remember, praise, and adore the
Lord; to share in the participation of his favors. The temporal
state of the brotherhood is not overlooked in these meetings.
Contributions are made for the necessities of saints. The deacons
are acquainted, and, through him, the whole fraternity, with the
circumstances of all. Under its wise and wholesome discipline
care is taken that every member capable of labor, work with his
own hands diligently at some honest calling. The contracting of
heavy and oppressive debts is proscribed. No brother is allowed
to enthrall himself nor others in any sort of worldly speculations
which incurs either anxiety on his part or inconvenience to others. The aged, feeble, and helpless are taken care of by the brethren. The indolent, slothful, and bad economist are censured, admonished, and reformed, or excluded. The Lord's table is constantly furnished. The bishops' wants and necessities always
supplied, and no one deprived of any necessary good. There are
persons fitted for every service; and those who attend continually on this good service, become eminent in the faith, and after

refreshing others are again in turn refreshed themselves. In this view of the deacon's office, we cannot but concur with the sayings and views of the primitive fathers who considered the deacons as the treasurers of the congregation, and as appointed to the service of tables, namely, the Lord's table, the poor's table, and the bishop's table.

Chapter Fifteen

Unreserved Devotion to God [31]

There is no trait in the character of the Savior more clearly marked, more forcibly exhibited in the memoirs of his life, than his unreserved devotion to the will of his Father and his God. How often do we hear him say, "I came not to do my own will, but the will of him that sent me." "It is my meat and my drink to do the will of him that sent me, and to accomplish his work." The motto of his life was sung by David in these words: "To do thy will, O God, I delight." An unfeigned and unreserved submission to, a perfect acquiescence in, and a fixed unalterable determination to do, the will of the Most High, is the standard of true devotion, and the rule and measure of true happiness. Whence, let me ask, arose this devotion to the will of the Father in our Lord and Savior? We answer, because he knew the Father. He knew that God is, and was, and ever will be love, and he received every expression of his will, whether pleasing or displeasing to flesh and blood, as an exhibition of God's love. He knew too that there was no love like the love of God, either in nature or degree. The love of God is a love emanating from, incorporated with, and measured by, an infinite wisdom, and omniscience. Human affection is often misplaced and misdirected, because of human ignorance and human weakness. The love of some men is much greater than that of others, because of the strength of their natural endowments. But as the wisdom and knowledge of God are searchable, so his love never can be misplaced, misdirected, never can be measured, nor circumscribed.

---

[31] "A Restoration of the Ancient Order of Things — No. XX," *Christian Baptist* Vol. 5, No. 1 (1827).

It is perfect in nature, and in nature it is wisdom, power, and goodness combined. In degree it cannot be conceived of by a finite mind, nor expressed in our imperfect vehicles of thought. It passeth all created understanding. It has a height without top, and a depth without bottom. Every oracle of God is a manifestation of it. As the electric fluid pervades the earth and all bodies upon it, but is invisible to the eye and imperceptible to the touch; but when drawn to a focus in a cloud by its law of attraction, and when it is discharged to another body which requires more of it than the point from which it emanated, it assumes a new form, and a new name, and becomes visible to the eye, and its voice is heard. Every expression of the will of God, every commandment of God, is only drawing to a certain point, and giving form and efficacy to his love. It then becomes visible—it is then audible. We see it—we hear it—we feel it.

The very term *devotion* has respect to the will of another. A devoted or devout man is a man who has respect to the will of God. When a person is given up to the will of any person, or to his own will, he is devoted to that person or to himself. But as the term *devout* is used in religion, we may say that every man is more or less devout, according to his regard to the will of God expressed in his holy oracles. The Savior was perfectly so, and he is and ever shall be the standard of perfect devotion. Not an item of the will of God found in the volume of the old book written concerning him, that he did not do, or submit to; not a single commandment did he receive in person from his Father which he did not perfectly acquiesce in and obey. He was then perfectly *devout.*

Now, in proportion as men are regenerated, they are like him. Faith always purifies the heart. A pure is an unmixed heart, that is, a heart singly fixed upon the will of God. The regenerated are therefore devout, or devoted to the will of God, and the unregenerated care nothing about it. Now everyone that is devout, or devoted to the will of God, will continually be inquiring into the will of God. Hence his oracles will always be their meditation. Every regenerated man will therefore be devout, devoted to the revealed will or God, will seek to know, and understand, and practice them; therefore, every regenerated man will be a friend and advocate of the ancient order of things, in the church of the Living God, because that order was according to the will of God, and every departure from it is according to the will of man. There is not a proposition in Euclid susceptible of a clearer or fuller demonstration than this: *Every regenerated man must be devoted* to *the ancient order of things in the church of God* – Provided it be granted as a postulatum, *that the ancient order of things was consonant* to *the will of the Most High.* A mind not devoted to the whole will of God, revealed in the New Book, is unregenerate. He that does not obey God in everything, obeys him in nothing. Hearken to this similitude –

A householder who had one son and many servants, was about to depart on a long journey to a distant country; he called his son into his presence, and said to him, my son, I am about to be absent for a long time; you know I have a vineyard, and an olive yard, and an orchard of various kinds of fruit. These I have cultivated with great care, and have kept my servants employed in fencing, and in cultivating each of them with equal labor and care. I now give them and my servants into your care and management until my return, and I now command you to have each of them fenced, and pruned, and cultivated as you have seen me do, and at my return I will reward you for your fidelity. He departed. His son calls all the servants together and having a predilection to the grape above every other fruit, he assembles them all in the vineyard. He improves the fences; he erects his wine vat and bestows great labor and attention on the pruning and cultivating the vines. They bring forth abundantly; but his attention and the labor of the servants are so much engrossed in the vineyard, that the olive yard and orchard are forgotten and neglected. In process of time his father returns. He finds his vineyard well enclosed, highly cultivated, and richly laden with the choicest grapes. But on visiting his orchard and olive yard he finds the enclosures broken down, the trees undressed and browsed upon by all the beasts of the field. He calls his son, who hangs his head in his presence. His father asks, why is it, my son, that my olive yard and orchard are so neglected and destroyed, while my vineyard flourishes, and is laden with fruit? Father, said he, I have always thought the grape was the most delicious of all fruit, the most salutary, as it cheered the heart of God and man, and therefore the worthiest of constant care and cultivation—I therefore bestowed all my attention upon it. His father rejoined, Unfaithful child! it was not my pleasure, my mind, nor my will, then, which guided you—but your own inclination. Had you preferred anything else to the vineyard, for the same reason that you neglected my orchard and olive yard, you would have neglected it. I thank you not for your cultivation of the vine, because, in doing this, you consulted not my pleasure, but your own. Undutiful son, depart from my presence! I will disinherit you and give my possessions to a stranger.

So it is with everyone who is zealous for keeping up one institution of the King of kings, while he is regardless of the others.

Some Baptists are extremely devoted to immersion. They have read all the baptisms on record in the New Testament, and beginning at the Jordan they end at the city of Philippi, in the bath in the Roman prison. The *ancient* mode and nothing else will please their taste. Away with your sprinkling and pouring, and baby-ism! The authority of the Great King is described in glowing colors. The importance of implicit obedience is extolled, and the great utility of keeping his commands is set forth in language which cannot be mistaken. But when the ancient mode of observing the Lord's Day, or of breaking bread is called up to their attention, they fall asleep. The authority of the Great King will scarcely make them raise their heads or open their eyes. Implicit obedience now has no charms, and the utility of keeping his commands has no attractions for them. Such Baptists are not regenerated, that is, they are not devout — not devoted to the will of God. They seek to please themselves. Let such compare themselves with the son of the householder in the preceding parable. They have got a *Baptist conscience,* and not the conscience of the regenerate. A Baptist conscience hears the voice of God and regards his authority only where there is much water. But a regenerated mind and a Christian conscience hears the voice of God and regards his authority as much on every Lord's Day, or at the Lord's table, as on the monthly meeting, as at Enon, or in the desert of Gaza. Many, we fear, think they are pleasing and serving God, while they are pleasing and serving themselves. They think they are devout; but they are devoted to their own will. So is everyone who acknowledges anything to be the will of God, and yet refuses to do it.

Ah! remember, my friends, that all flesh is as grass, and all the glory of man; rabbinical, clerical, regal, is as the flower of the grass; the grass withereth, and the flower falleth down, but he that DOETH *the will of God abideth forever.* Ye doctors of divinity, who are doting about questions and fighting about straws, ye editors of religious journals, who are surfeiting the religious mind with your fulsome panegyrics upon those who second your views, and directing the public mind to objects lighter than vanity — remember that the will of Jehovah will stand forever, and that when "gems and monuments and crowns are moldered down to dust," he that does the will of God shall flourish in immortal youth. Go to work, then, and use your influence to restore the ancient order of things.

Chapter Sixteen

Songs (No. I) [32]

Being an extract from the preface to a new selection of psalms, hymns, and spiritual songs, about to be issued from this press.

Psalm and hymn singing, like every other part of Christian worship, has been corrupted by sectarianism. This demon, whose name is Legion, has possessed all our spirit, and given a wrong direction to almost all our religious actions. A consistent sectary not only contends for a few dry abstract opinions, nicknamed "articles of belief" or "essential points," but these he sings and prays with a zeal proportioned to the opposition made to them. How loud and how long does the Arminian sing his *free grace*, while he argues against the Calvinists' *sovereign* grace. And in what animating strains does the Calvinist sing of his *imputed righteousness* in the presence of the Arminian, who, he supposes, is seeking to be justified by his works. Annihilate these sects, and these hymns either die with them, or undergo a new modification. He that sings them in the spirit of the sect, pays homage to the idol of a party, but worships not the God of the whole earth. Were I asked for a good criterion of a sectarian spirit, I would answer, When a person derives more pleasure from the contemplation of a tenet because of the opposition made to it, than he would, did no such opposition exist; or when he is more opposed to a tenet because of the system to which it belongs or the people who hold it, than on account of its own innate meaning and tendency, he acts the sectary and not the

---

[32] "A Restoration of the Ancient Order of Things — No. XXI," *Christian Baptist* Vol. 5, No. 5 (1827).

Christian; and so of all predilections and antipathies, when they are created, guided, or controlled by anything extrinsic of the subject matter itself.

Our hymns are, for the most part, our creed in meter, while it appears in the prose form in our confessions. A Methodist sermon must be succeeded by a Methodist hymn and a Methodist mode of singing it. And so of the Presbyterian. There is little or no difference in any sect in this one particular. Even the Quaker is not singular here; for as he has no regular sermon he has no regular song, hymn, nor prayer. Those who have many frames and great vicissitudes of feeling sing and pray much about them; and those who are more speculative than practical, prefer exercises of intellect to those of the heart or affections.

The hymn book is as good an index to the brains and to the hearts of a people as the creed book; and scarce a "sermon is preached" which is not followed up by a corresponding hymn or song.

Does the preacher preach up Sinai instead of Calvary, Moses instead of Christ, to convince or convict his audience? Then he sings —

> "Awak'd by Sinai's awful sound,
> "My soul in bonds of guilt I found,
> "And knew not where to go;
> "O'erwhelm'd with sin, with anguish slain,
> "The sinner must be *born again,*
> "Or sink to endless woe."
> "When to the law I trembling fled,
> "It pour'd its curses on my head;
> "I no relief could find.
> *"This fearful truth* increas'd my pain,
> "The sinner must be *born again."*
> "Again did Sinai's thunder roll,
> "And guilt lay heavy on my soul,

148

> "A vast unwieldly load!
> "Alas! I read and saw it plain,
> "The sinner must be *born again,*
> "Or drink the wrath of God."

I know of nothing more anti-evangelical than the above verses; but they suit one of our law-convincing sermons, and the whole congregation must sing, suit or non-suit the one half of them. But to finish the climax, this exercise is called *praising* God.

But again—Does the preacher teach his congregation that the time and place when and where the sinner should be converted were decreed from all eternity? Then out of complaisance to the preacher the congregation must *praise* the Lord by singing—

> "Twas fix'd in God's eternal mind
> "When his dear sons should mercy find:
> "From everlasting he decreed
> *"When* every good should be convey'd."
> "Determin'd was the manner how
> "We should be brought the Lord to know;
> "Yea, he decreed the very place
> *Where* he would call us by his grace."

Is the absolute and unconditional perseverance of all the converted taught? Then, after sermon, all must sing—

> "Safe in the arms of Sovereign Love
> "We ever shall remain,
> "Nor shall the rage of earth or hell
> "Make thy dear counsels vain."
> "Not one of all the chosen race
> "But shall to heaven attain;
> "Partake on earth the purpos'd grace,
> "And then with Jesus reign."

But does the system teach that there are, and must necessarily be, *cold* and *dark* seasons in the experience of all Christians, and

149

that such only are true Christians who have their doubts, fears, glooms, and winters? Then the audience sings—

"Dear Lord, if, indeed, I am thine,
"If thou art my sun and my song,
"Say why do I languish and pine,
"And why are my winters so long!
"O drive these dark clouds from my sky,
"Thy soul-cheering presence restore,
"Or take me unto thee on high,
"Where winter and clouds are no more."

Once, and no more at present. Does the preacher affirm that there is some *private title* which each Christian must have independent of the *public promise, pledge,* and *oath* of the Almighty, given to everyone who flees for refuge to the hope set before us in the gospel, and that this *private title* is more or less dubious in law? Then his congregation must sing—

"When I can read my title clear
"To mansions in the skies,
"I'll bid farewell to every fear,
"And wipe my weeping eyes."

Queries for the thoughtful. 1. What *title* is this? 2. What would make it clearer? 3. Who issued this title? 4. Where is it filed? 5. Why does its dubiety forbid to part with every fear, and to banish tears? 6. Could you not make it more clear by instituting a new action, or course of action?

Without being prolix or irksome in filing objections to all these specimens of hymn singing, I shall mention but two or three: —

1. They are, in toto, contrary to the spirit and genius of the Christian religion.

2. They are unfit for any congregation, as but few in any one congregation can with regard to truth apply them to themselves.

3. They are an essential part of the corrupt systems of this day, and a decisive characteristic of the grand apostacy. But a farther development of this subject we postpone to our next.

Songs (No. II) [33]

Psalms, hymns, and spiritual songs, embrace the praises of Christians. Psalms are historic compositions, or poetic narratives. Hymns are odes of praise directly addressing the object of worship and declaring his excellencies and glorious works. Spiritual songs are such compositions as declare the sentiments derived from the revelations of God, and such as are adapted to communicate to others the views and feelings which God's revelations suggest. This we define them. The reasons of this distribution are not obvious to all, nor is it needful to go into a labored criticism to establish it, as the end will be gained much better by an attention to the classification we have made in this new selection of psalms, hymns, and spiritual songs, than by any *critique* independent of such a specimen. Our hymn books are, in general, a collection of everything under the sun in the form of religious rhyme. Not one in ten, or, perhaps, in twenty, of any selection, are usually sung by any individual from choice or approbation. And, indeed, the religious communities seem to be destitute of any fixed standard by which to judge of what is comely and suitable subject matter of social praise. As was said, the greater part conceive they ought to sing every notion, speculation, or opinion, which they can imagine to be orthodox; not apprehending that the object of sacred song is to raise and exalt our spirits by divine contemplations to the sublime in the worship of our adorable God and Father, by admiring and extolling

---

[33] "A Restoration of the Ancient Order of Things — No. XXII," *Christian Baptist* Vol. 5, No. 6 (1828).

facts extrinsic of our conjectures or notions about them. But this is not all; every heretical or schismatic dogma is sung, as well as preached; and instead of *praising* God, we are often *scolding* men who differ from us. For even prayer has been abused to this end. Often have I seen a prayer to be dictated by the presence of someone in the congregation; and thus, all the congregation were doing homage to the zeal of the preacher, who was praying in relation to some influential heretic as he conceived. I knew a preacher who got into a violent controversy with another, because of an insult he gave him in prayer. And not long since a preacher has been called to order by the legislature of the first state in the union in point of population, for an insult to the nation while praying as chaplain for the legislature. This spirit, which on many other occasions manifests itself in prayer, is equally at work in the department of religious praise. So that all our contests about religion get into our prayers and songs.

Let us analyze a few more specimens. There has been a controversy of long standing about faith. One hymn extols faith in the following words: —

"Faith—'tis a precious grace
Where'er it is bestow'd!
It boasts of a celestial birth,
And is the gift of God.

Jesus it owns a King,
An all-atoning Priest;
It claims no merit of its own,
But looks for all in Christ.

To him it leads the soul
When filled with deep destress,
Flies to the fountain of his blood,
And trusts his righteousness.

152

Since 'tis thy work alone,
And that divinely free,
Lord, send the spirit of thy Son
To work this faith in me."

Waving any discussion upon the propriety of singing praises to *faith* instead of the *Lord*, I proceed to observe that in singing the above verses we are boasting against those who are supposed to maintain that faith is not of a celestial birth, and not the gift of God. In the conclusion the singer is made to act a singular part—first to declare that he believes that Jesus is a King, an all-atoning Priest; that faith leers the soul to him, flies to the fountain of his blood, and trusts his righteousness; and yet, after having sung all this, he represents himself as destitute of such a faith as he has been singing, and prays for the spirit of Jesus Christ to *work* this faith in him! How the same person can sing the three first verses and the last one in this hymn I know not, unless they sing as a parrot speaks, without regard to the meaning. To convert the above sentiments into plain prose, it reads thus: "I believe that faith is a precious grace, the gift of God, of celestial origin. I believe that Jesus is King and an all-atoning Priest; that his righteousness is worthy of my trust, and his blood purges me from sin—No, I don't believe this; but, Lord, send the spirit of thy Son, who I believe works this grace in men's hearts; and as I don't yet believe, work this faith in me!!

"Come Holy Spirit, heavenly dove,
With all thy quick'ning powers;
Kindle a flame of sacred love
In these cold hearts of ours.

Look how we grovel here below,
Fond of these trifling toys;
Our souls can neither fly, nor go,

To reach eternal joys."

These verses, as well as the general scope of this song, are not accordant with the spirit of the Christian religion. The Holy Spirit is always represented as the author of all goodness in us and is not to be addressed by men as though they, without it, could say that Jesus is Lord, or, without it, breathe forth a spiritual desire. But here dead "cold hearts" are represented as panting after the Holy Spirit. — But not only does the nature of the Christian religion, which represents the Father as the terminating end of all Christian worship, the Son as the only mediator between the Father and us, and the Holy Spirit as the immediate agent or author of all goodness in us. Not only, I say, does the nature of the religion itself, to those who understand it, teach the impropriety of direct addresses to the Holy Spirit; but this species of address is absolutely unauthorized by any Prophet or Apostle, by any oracle of God, commandment or precedent in the sacred books — For from the beginning of Genesis to the end of Revelation, no man — patriarch, Jew, nor Christian; prophet, priest, nor Apostle, ever did address the Holy Spirit directly in prayer or praise. They pray *for* the Holy Spirit, but never *to* it. Thus, Paul desired that the love of the Father, the grace of the Lord Jesus, and the communion of the Holy Spirit, might be with the saints. This hymn, then, is not only contrary to the genius of the New Covenant, but un-commanded and unprecedented in the book of God. This I asserted to an association about ten years ago, which caused an old preacher to search the whole Bible through to disprove it. In something less than a year afterwards he wrote me he had found me in an error — for he had found an authority for this hymn. It was, he said, in the book of Canticles, where it saith, "Awake, O North wind, and blow thou, South, upon my garden," etc. But the old gentleman hath not, to this day, decided whether the Holy Spirit was in the North or in the

South wind, and therefore, as yet nothing has been adduced to show the assertion unfounded.

Chapter Seventeen

Church Discipline [34]

"Let all things be done decently and in order," is a favorite saying, though seldom regarded with suitable respect by those who are wont to be charmed with the sound of the words. The two extremes in all associations, as respects government or rule, are despotism and anarchy. In some religious establishments there is, on the part of the rulers, an unrelenting and absolute tyranny, and on the part of the ruled, a passive servility, as if non-resistance and passive obedience were the cardinal virtues in a good sectarian. In other religious institutions there is, on the part of the rulers, no attribute of ecclesiastical authority, and on the part of the ruled, there is the most licentious equality, which recognizes not either the letter or the spirit of subordination. These doubtless are the extremes between which lie the temperate zone, or the *"media tutissima via,"* the safe middle way.

But there are extremes not only in one department of congregational proceedings, but in all. Let us take an example from some popular measures: — Here in this hierarchy "the *canaille"* or mass of the community have nothing to say or do in the creation of their teachers or rulers. They are neither permitted to judge nor to decide upon their attainments before they are invested with the office of public instructors. But there, in yonder religious establishment, every man, woman, or child, is constituted into a competent tribunal, and made supreme judge of the attainments of the person and feel themselves competent to invest him with the office of a religious instructor, without further

---

[34] "A Restoration of the Ancient Order of Things — No. XXIII," *Christian Baptist* Vol. 5, No. 8 (1828).

ceremony than their own unanimity or majority. For instance, here is a church of thirty members, ten males and twenty females. One of the ten is, by some of the twenty-nine, supposed to be qualified to become a preacher, or, as they understand it, a public instructor. Now, of the nine males and twenty females, it so happens that there are six matrons who can read intelligibly the New Testament; and of the males there are about four of what might be called plain common sense, who can barely understand a piece of plain narrative composition. But among them, such as they are, they decide that AB is competent to be a public instructor, and they forthwith commission him to go into all the world, and preach the gospel unto every creature. Now the question is, are they to be condemned or justified who consider this man legitimately introduced into the world as a teacher of religion? Is any other society bound to credit his pretensions, or to receive him *bona fide*[35] as a legally authorized teacher of the Christian religion, and ruler in the Christian church? Remember the question is not, Had the twenty females and the nine males, by and with his own consent, a right to create, appoint, and ordain him a ruler and teacher over themselves; but whether they have reason or revelation on their side, when they introduce him to all the world, as a regularly initiated minister, or ambassador, or teacher of, and for Christ? That any society, politically considered, have a right to manage their own affairs as they please, is at once readily admitted; that any ecclesiastical community have a right to govern themselves by whatever laws they please, as far as the state jurisdiction extends, is also conceded; but that any society has any right to frame any regulations for its own government on Christian principles, is what we cannot so readily subscribe. But without being further

---

[35] Or, "genuinely."

tedious about extremes, having simply shown that there are extremes, and that we are prone to run *into* them on both hands, I will proceed to my object in this part of my series of essays on the ancient order of things.

As we have many volumes on church government and church discipline; and as the Episcopal, Presbyterial, and Independent, all have claimed a *jus divinum*,[36] we cannot be expected to have much *new* on the subject, or to have little regard to the merits of the questions which they have with so much warmth debated. We wish, however, while we write, to forget all that we have ever read or heard on this subject, save what the apostolic writings contain upon such topics. As we prefer perspicuity to all other attributes of good writing, we proceed to state —

First, that as the church, or congregation, or assembly, (as it is expressed by all these names,) is repeatedly called a *kingdom* — the kingdom of God, and the kingdom of heaven, it is fairly to be presumed, from the terms themselves, that the government under which the church is placed, is *an absolute monarchy*. There cannot be a *kingdom* unless there be a *king*. They are correlative terms, and the one necessarily supposes the existence of the other. But we are not left to inference; for it was not only foretold expressly that "the government would be upon his shoulders;" but he claims absolute dominion in express and unequivocal terms and lays all his disciples under the strict *in*junction of unreserved submission. All authority in the Universe is given to him — "Therefore, *kiss the Son.*" – "*I* have placed my *king* upon mount Zion." — "He shall *reign* over the house of Israel, his people, forever." On *this,* as a first principle, I found all my views of what *is* commonly called *church government.* All the churches on earth that Christ has ever acknowledged as his, are so many communities constituting one kingdom, of which he is the head

---

[36] Or, "divine law."

and sovereign. — The congregation or community in Rome, in Corinth, in Philippi, in Ephesus, etc., were so many distinct communities as respected their component members or individuals, but these were all under one and the same government, as the different counties or corporations in the state of Virginia are all component parts of the state, and under the same government. In every congregation or community of Christians the persons that are appointed by the Great King to rule, act pretty much in the capacity of our civil magistrates; or in other words, they have only to see that the laws are obeyed but have no power or right to legislate in any one instance for any one purpose. The constitution and laws of this kingdom are all of divine origin and authority, having emanated from the bosom, and having been promulged in the name of the Universal King.

There is no democracy or aristocracy in the governmental arrangements of the church of Jesus Christ. The citizens are all volunteers when they enlist under the banners of the Great King, and so soon as they place themselves in the ranks, they are bound to implicit obedience in all the institutes and laws of their sovereign. So that there is no putting the question to vote whether they shall obey any particular law or injunction. Their rulers or bishops have to give an account of their administration and have only to see that the laws are known and obeyed, and hence proceed all the exhortations in the epistles to the communities addressed to submit to their rulers, as those who watch for their souls, and as those who must give an account of their administration.

This subject, it has appeared to me, is very little or very imperfectly understood in many congregations, and their meetings for church discipline are generally conducted in such a way as to divest everyone in the assembly of every attribute of authority, and to place every one in the character of an interpreter of the law: and if not legislators, at least, they are all *executors* of it. But of this more hereafter.

On Discipline of the Church (No. I) [37]

LETTERS TO R.B. SEMPLE — *Letter III*

Brother Semple,

Dear Sir — You say that "church government is obviously left by the Bible for the exercise of much discretion." How this can be I cannot conjecture. Whatever is left for the exercise of much discretion is obviously a discretionary thing. If, therefore, church government be a matter obviously of human discretion, I see not how any form of church government, though principally of human contrivance, such as the Papistical or Episcopalian, can be condemned. Each of these forms takes something from the Bible and much from human discretion. We may think that what their discretion adopts is very far from being discreet; but in condemning their taste, we cannot censure them as transgressors of law; for obviously where there is no law, there is no transgression. If there be no divine law enjoining any form of church-government; if there be no divinely authorized platform exhibited in the Bible, then why have the Baptists contended for the independent form, except they suppose that they have more discretion than their neighbors?

---

[37] "A Restoration of the Ancient Order of Things — No. XXIV," *Christian Baptist* Vol. 5, No. 10 (1828).

But what you call *"church government"* may, perhaps, be entirely a matter of human discretion, such as fixing the time of day at which the church shall meet; also, the hour of adjournment; the place of meeting, whether in a stone, brick, or wooden building; the shape and size of their house, and the seats and conveniences thereof. On these items the Bible, indeed, says but little. Or, perhaps, brother Semple, under the terms "church government," you may place synods, councils, associations; the duties of moderators and clerks; rules of decorum, and parliamentary proceedings in deliberative bodies; all of which some think as necessary to the well-being of the church as "the scaffolding is to the house." If you embrace all these items, and other kindred ones, in your idea of church government, I perfectly agree with you in one part of your assertion, that the Bible says little or nothing on such matters; but I do not say that they are all left to human discretion, and therefore I cannot flatter myself into the opinion that the synods and advisory councils of Presbyterians and independents are innocent matters of human discretion!!

You have, no doubt, brother Semple, often observed, and remarked to others, that a majority of the disputes in religion have originated from not defining the terms or using the same words as representatives of the same ideas. I have often said that the chief advantage which mathematical demonstration has above moral or philological proof, is owing to a greater precision in the terms used in the former, than in the latter species of reasoning. Many an angry and verbose controversy has been dissipated by the definition of a single term; and the angry disputants, after they had exhausted themselves, finally agreed that they misunderstood one another. When you say that "church government is obviously left by the Bible for the exercise of much discretion," I am led to suspect that you attach a meaning to these terms quite different from that which I and many others attach to them. The reason I think so is because I am puzzled to find a definition of them that will accord with your assertion.

By *"church government"* I understand the government of the church, which the Bible teaches is upon the shoulders of Immanuel. He placed the twelve apostles upon twelve thrones and commanded the nations to obey them. I find, therefore, that the Lord Jesus is the Governor, and the twelve apostles under him, sitting upon twelve thrones, constitute the *government* of the church of Jesus Christ. I know that synods and advisory councils have a right to govern voluntary associations, which owe their origin to the will of men; but in the church of Jesus the twelve apostles reign. Jesus the King, the glorious and mighty Lord, gave them their authority. The church is a congregation of disciples meeting in one place—an assembly of regenerated persons, who have agreed to walk together under the guidance of Jesus Christ. Hence, they are to be governed by his laws. All the exhortations concerning temper, behavior, and discourse found in the apostolic writings, in all their addresses to the congregations after the day of Pentecost, constitute *the government of the church,* properly so called. When all the apostolic injunctions, such as those concerning the government of the thoughts, the tongue, and the hands of Christians are regarded, then the church is under the government of the Lord. Laws, moral and religious (*i.e.* laws governing men's moral and religious actions) are the only laws which Jesus deigns to enact. He legislates not upon matters of mere policy, or upon bricks, stones, and logs of timber. He says nothing about moderators, clerks, and parliamentary decorum; but upon moral and religious behavior he is incomparably sublime. He enacts nothing upon the confederation of churches, of delegate meetings, or any matter of temporal and worldly policy. Hence, they strain out a gnat and swallow an elephant, who complain there is no law authorizing the building of meeting

163

houses, and yet find a warrant for a "state convention" or a religious convent, college, or seminary of learning. The matter of church government which was discussed at Westminster was never mentioned by the Lord nor his apostles. When I hear Independents, Presbyterians, and Episcopalians, contending about their different forms of church government, I think of the three travelers contending about the color of the chameleon: One declared it was *blue*; another affirmed it was *green*; a third swore it was *black*; and yet, when the creature was produced, all saw it was WHITE.

As some of the wisest philosophers of the present century have discarded what has been improperly called "moral philosophy" from the circle of sciences, because it has no foundation in nature; so methinks the subject of "church government" and the whole controversy about it, in the popular sense of these terms, might safely be sent back to the cloisters of the church of Rome, whence it came. Let the moral and religious government of the institutes and exhortations addressed to disciples in their individual and social capacities be regarded, and there is no need of your by-laws or borough regulations.

The decorum of a public assembly is well defined, both in the sacred oracles, and in the good sense of all persons of reflection. And if disciples met not for "doing business," but for edification, prayer, and praise, or discipline, they will never need any other platform or rules of decorum than the writings of Paul, Peter, James, and John. But if you, brother Semple, will have the daughter attired like her mother; or if you wish any sect to become respectable in the eyes of those acquainted with the fashions in London and Rome, you must have sectarian colleges under the patronage of churches, and churches under the patronage of associations, and associations under the patronage of state conventions, and state conventions under the patronage of a constitution, creed, and book of discipline, called "church government." And the nigher these latter approximate to the see of Canterbury, or that of Rome, the more useful and honorable will they appear in the estimation of such Christians as are deemed orthodox in the District of Columbia.

I feel very conscious that the less you and other good Christians say about "church government," in the popular sense, the better for its safety with the people, who have contended for something, they know not *what,* under this name. And just as certain am I, that, if the laws governing moral and religious demeanor, in the epistles, are regarded, as they must be by all who are really taught of God, there will be found no need for our bylaws or regulations in the congregation of the faithful, not even in cases of discipline when transgressors present themselves.

Brother Semple, when I hear you call the church *"a corporation,"* the Bible its *"charter,"* and the creed its *"by-laws;"* or, perhaps, you make the essay on discipline its by-laws: I say, when I hear a Baptist Bishop of such eminence, in the state of Virginia, in the reign of Grace 1828, thus express himself, I feel almost constrained to take up my parable and sing —

> *"By Babel's streams we sat and wept,*
> *"When Zion we thought on;*
> *"In midst thereof we hang'd our harps*
> *"The willow trees upon."*
> *I hope to be still more explicit in my next.*
> *Yours with all respect,*

EDITOR

On the Discipline of the Church (No. II) [38]

Sundry letters have been received on the subjects of associations, conferences, laying on of hands, family worship; all either objecting to some things advanced in this work, or seeking further expositions and elucidations of arguments already offered in this work on these subjects. These letters are too numerous and too long to be inserted in any reasonable time. We have therefore concluded to prosecute our iniquities on the order and discipline of the church and intend meeting all these objections in the course of our essays as they may naturally occur. In the meantime we proceed to some matters of greater importance in the discipline of the church, and must solicit a due degree of patience on the part of our correspondents.

All matters of church discipline are either private injuries or public offences; sometimes designated "public and private offences," or "public and private trespasses." Private injuries, trespasses, or offences are those which in the first instance directly affect individuals and are known only to individuals. For a *private* injury or trespass, so soon as it is generally known, becomes a *public* offence. Now the object of the precepts in the New Testament concerning private trespasses, is to prevent their becoming public offences; and that by healing them when only felt and known by the parties; — the person injured, and he that commits the trespass. The directions given by the Savior in Matthew 18 belong exclusively to this class of trespasses. Thus, according to this law, if A injure B, either by word or deed addressed to him alone B, who is injured privately tells A the injury he has re-

[38] "A Restoration of the Ancient Order of Things — No. XXV," *Christian Baptist* Vol. 6, No. 1 (1828).

ceived from him; and if, after expostulating with him, A confesses his fault and professes repentance, or if he explain the matter to the satisfaction of B, the affair ends, because the parties are reconciled to each other. But if neither acknowledgment, explanation, confession, or repentance can be elicited, and B still feels himself aggrieved, he calls upon his brethren, D, E, and F, and in their presence states his grievance. They also hear what A has to offer. After having the case fairly before them, they are prepared to advise, expostulate, explain, and judge righteously. Now if A hears them, is convinced by them, and can be induced to make reparation either by word or deed for the trespass inflicted, or if they can effect a reconciliation between the parties, the matter terminates, and is divulged no farther. But if A cannot or will not hear or be persuaded by D, E, and F, but despise their interposition, expostulation, or advice, B must acquaint the congregation with the fact that A has trespassed against him. Then the congregation are to inquire, not into the nature of the trespass, but whether he have taken the proper steps. He answers in the affirmative, and calls upon D, E, and F, for the proof. On the testimony of D, E, and F, every word is established or confirmed. The congregation being satisfied with the standing of D, E, and F, and having heard their testimony, proceed to admonish, expostulate with, and entreat A to make reparation to his brother B. If he is then persuaded and B is reconciled to him, the matter terminates, and both are retained; but if otherwise, and A will not hear nor regard, but despise the congregation, then he is to be excluded. It does not appear that the original quarrel, misunderstanding, or trespass is to be told to the whole congregation, and they made to sit together in judgment upon it. If this were so, there was no necessity for having anything established upon the testimony of D, E, and F. Whereas the Savior said that, by the testimony of two or three witnesses, everything may be ascertained or established. Nothing would be ascertained or established if A and B are permitted now to disturb the congregation by a recital of the whole matter; for in this way, it is more likely to distract and injure the peace and harmony of the congregation, than to reconcile the parties. But, in case that A complains of injustice in the case, then the congregation appoint two or three others to hear and judge the matter; and upon their declaration to the congregation the matter terminates. But it does not appear, either from what the Lord enjoins in the passage before cited, or what Paul lays down in 1 Corinthians 6, that the nature of the trespass is to be told. "When you have secular seats of judicature make to sit on them who are least (ironically for most) esteemed in the church." *"Is there not among you* a wise man, *not even one* WHO SHALL BE ABLE TO DECIDE BETWEEN HIS BRETHREN."

The practice of telling all private scandals, trespasses, and offences to the whole congregation, is replete with mischief. It often alienates members of the church from each other, and brings feuds and animosities into the congregation, and it is very seldom that a promiscuous congregation of men, women, and children can decide so unanimously or so wisely upon such cases, as two or three either called upon by the parties or appointed by the congregation. This moreover appears to be the true import of all the laws upon this subject in the New Testament. On Matthew 18, the only question which can arise of any importance, is, whether B is to tell the original trespass to the whole congregation, or whether he is to tell the fact that A has injured him and will not reform or make reparation. I think the original and the English version authorize the latter, namely, that he is to tell the congregation that A had trespassed against him, and would not hear D, E and F. This is the immediate antecedent to the command, *"Tell the congregation."* But on this I would not lay so much stress, as upon the other regulations and laws found in the volume concerning trespasses, and upon the necessary consequences arising from each method of procedure. Very often, indeed, the affair is of a nature as ought not to be told, and could not be told in a public assembly of Christians without violating some law or rule which the volume enjoins; and not unfrequently are whole congregations distracted by the injudicious, and, as we think, unscriptural practice, of telling the whole congregation a matter of which but a few of them are able to form correct views. And such is the common weakness of the great majority of members of any community, that but few are able to judge profoundly in cases requiring the exercise of much deliberation.

On the Discipline of the Church (No. III) [39]

In our last we wrote on the evangelical law relative to private offences. We are now to call the attention of our readers to public offences. And before opening the law and the testimony on the treatment of such offences, we will occupy the present number in treating of these offences in general.

Whatever action, or course of conduct, contrary either to the letter or spirit of either the moral or religious injunctions or restrictions delivered by the Savior or his Apostles, is an offence against the gospel order and the author of it; and in proportion as such offences are known, either to the society or the world at large, are they more or less public; and, as such, to be examined, judged, and reprobated, according to the law of the Great King.

---

[39] "A Restoration of the Ancient Order of Things — No. XXVI," *Christian Baptist* Vol. 6, No. 2 (1828).

After speaking in terms so general, it becomes expedient to descend to particulars. And here let it be noted that too little attention is paid to some infractions of the evangelical institution, and an extravagant emphasis laid upon others, as if, they exclusively merited the attention of Christian communities, were the only actions to be inquired into according to scriptural authority. Such reasoners ought to be sent to the Apostle James to learn logic. He teaches that he that violates any one commandment, sins against the authority and will of the lawgiver, as well as he that transgresses all the laws of the empire. For he that said, *"Do not commit adultery,"* said also, *"Do not steal."* Now if you commit no adultery, yet if you steal, you are a transgressor. So reasons James the Apostle. Now according to this logic, let us attend to some offences or public trespasses very commonly not submitted to discipline in this latitudinarian age. And in the first place, let us attend to *detraction, slander,* or *evil speaking.* I do not mean to confine my remarks to that species of slander of which civil laws take cognizance, nor to those gross detractions which the different codes of ecclesiastic law take notice of but to what, in the judgment of the New Testament, is as really and as truly slander, detraction, and evil speaking, as those instances punished by law.

Every insinuation, inuendo, hint, allusion, or comparison, which is calculated or intended to diminish aught from the reputation or good name of any person; brother, or alien, is, in the discriminating morality and purity of the New Testament, accounted slander, detraction, or evil speaking. And here we may observe that the terms *evil speaking* are generic, and include every word and sentence, the meaning or design of which is calculated to do injury to the reputation of others. *Slander* is a species of evil speaking, and imparts false and foul imputations, or falsely ascribes to others reproachful actions incompatible with good character. *Detraction simply* derogates and defames, either by denying the merits of another, or subtracting from them. In this age and country *evil speaking* is as fashionable as lasciviousness was in Corinth. Our political papers at this time are rather vehicles of slander, than heralds of intelligence; and these feed and pamper a taste for slander and detraction, which is more likely to be the first trait of a national character, so soon as we can form one, than any other we can think of. I could wish that the same character was not likely to be merited by some of our *religious* print, whose avowed object is to subserve the spread of evangelical principles and practices throughout the land. Where slander and detraction are the order of the day in the public walks of life, it is difficult to keep this great evil out of the church and from the fireside of Christian circles.

Political and religious sects and parties, and the necessary rival interests to which they give rise, are the true causes of this awful deterioration of morals, both in church and state. Now if slander and detraction are as real infractions of the law of the great King as murder and theft, (and we must think they are) it is difficult to decide whether any nation or any people are more rapidly degenerating than the good citizens of the American Republics. It is the more difficult to resist this contagion because of its almost universal prevalence, and few appear conscious either of the enormity of the evil, or of what constitutes it. Even *"ministers of religion,"* as they are fashionably called, seem not to think that more than the tithe of their public sermons are religious slander or detraction. Nor is this sin confined to one sect either in church or state. Society is working itself into such a state as to make aspersions, defamations, and slander necessary to political health. And what is still worse, the *"religious presses."* *Controlled* by good and religious men, are giving countenance and encouragement to this pernicious custom. Insomuch that one-sided representations, innuendos, and detractions are supposed to be expedient for the maintenance of the popular plans and benevolent undertakings of the good men of the earth.

Men have their political and ecclesiastical idols; and these they worship not only with incessant adulations, but they offer them whole burnt offerings of the fame of their rivals. They seem to think no sacrifice is so acceptable to the idol of their party, as the good name of his competitor. The morning and the evening sacrifices of the Jews were not more regularly attended on in the tabernacles of Israel, than are the hecatombs of defamation and scandal in the temples of rival interests. No public nor private virtue can shield its possessor from the shafts of envy, and the calumnies of intrigue, should he be so unfortunate as to be nominated for any distinction amongst his peers. That moment his promotion is named, every restraint laid upon the tongue and the pen is withdrawn; and he stands a naked target upon a hill, to be pierced with the arrows of slander from every point in his horizon. He stands as a criminal upon a pillory, unprotected by law, unguarded by the sanctions of religion and morality. No man feels himself a sinner when he robs him of his good name, and as remorseless as the licensed hangman, he devotes him to destruction. So appears the state of things in the present crisis; yet but few seem to think that the evil is of much magnitude or consider it in any other light than a tax which must be paid into the revenue of the Temple of Fame. And yet methinks the life and the public services of a Washington or a Moses, protracted to the age of a Methuselah, could not atone for the guilt contracted in the present campaign for a four-year magistracy in these United States.

But whither am I straying from the subject before me! I only intended to observe, that so popular is the evil of which we complain, that it has become less offensive to our feelings, and we have become less conscious of its malignity; so that in religious, as well as in political society, it has become quite a matter of course, or a subject of easy endurance, if not of perfect forbearance. And even Christians seem to feel little (if any) compunction when they are whispering, backbiting, evil surmising, and suspicioning one against another. Judgments well informed and tender consciences recoil at the very thought of derogating from the good name of any one whom the law of love embraces as a fellow Christian. Christianity puts us upon quite a different course; it teaches us to esteem another better than ourselves; it extols that love which hides a multitude of sins, and ranks all detractions, slanders, and envy the root of this accursed fruit, amongst the works of the flesh, and associates the actors with Satan the accuser, and his kindred spirits bound over to the day of righteous retribution. Everything incompatible with the most cordial affection, is incompatible with the relation subsisting in the church of Christ; the nearest and the dearest, as well as the most permanent relation known on earth. The second birth introduces all into one family, one brotherhood, one inheritance, one eternal relation, which neither time, nor distance, nor death itself can destroy. In this relation, the highest pleasure is to see all honorable, irreproachable, and of exalted purity. It prompts us to draw the vail of forgetfulness over the defects, and to hide the faults we see in our brethren. It constrains the whole brotherhood to take cognizance of the person who, by a hint, inuendo, or allusion, defames any one they have confided in, and honored as a Christian brother. It constitutes the good name of each public property and can view in no other light then in that of a thief or a robber, the person who steals away a jot or tittle of the good character of any one of the sacred fraternity. Whenever this ceases to be the character of any religious society, they have fallen from their first love, and have lost the highest ornament which adorns Christian character. And here let us pause for the present.

On the Discipline of the Church (No. IV) [40]

Our last essay under this head was rather to point out some of those moral evils which call for the discipline of the congregation, than to develop the procedure of the congregation in relation to public offences. We spoke of some aberrations from the law of Christ, very generally overlooked in the discipline of the church. We shall continue this subject in the present essay. We ought first to know the law of our king before we presume to execute it.

In our last we treated almost exclusively of *evil speaking* in its genuine import. Very nearly allied to this, and an evil almost as general, is that of breach of promises and covenants amongst the professors of the present day. This is an evil of very serious magnitude and of alarming extent amongst our cotemporaries. The foundation of this evil will, we presume, be found in the cupidity, avarice, or commercial spirit of this age and country. The propensity for contracting debts, and of risking largely on contingencies, and the want of a due estimate of the solemnity of a promise or covenant, constitute the root of this desolating evil. It has become almost fashionable in society to excuse delinquencies and to apologize for the breach of solemn engagements by attributing it to the hardness or un-propitiousness of what we call *the times*. Mankind is ever wont to blame their sins on anything but themselves. There is no necessity for the disciples of him whose kingdom is not of this world, to incur such hazards or risk such responsibilities as the children of this world do, in their desires to amass treasures upon earth, or to follow in the train of pompous vanities which allure those whose eyes have

---

[40] "A Restoration of the Ancient Order of Things — No. XXVII," *Christian Baptist* Vol. 6, No. 3 (1828).

never been raised from earth to heaven. The disposition thus to conform to the world, argues very forcibly that professors have not found that in Jesus Christ which fills their hearts; or which they found in him, who for his excellencies accounted all things but dregs that they might attain unto that perfection in him which the resurrection of the dead will disclose. If we see a lady much abroad and seldom at home, we must conclude her happiness is not so much at home as abroad; or if we see a gentleman more attentive to other ladies than his wife, and more in their company, we are forced to conclude he finds not that in his wife which in his marriage covenant he professed to have found. In the same way we reason when we see a Christian laboring to acquire those earth-born distinctions which exclusively engross the attention of the sons of earth. If we see him as eager in the chase as they, we suspect he has not found in his profession that which he professed to have found when he made a formal surrender of himself to the Lord of life.

But lest we should stray from our subject, we must say that the whole system of speculation, of asking and giving securities, of incurring debts beyond the most obvious means to pay in any contingency which may be supposed, are just as opposite to the spirit and tendency of Christianity as theft, lying, and slander. Hence no Christian can be prosecuted at law in any such case, or, indeed, in any other case; but it behooves the congregation to examine his conduct whether he have been justly or unjustly prosecuted in the case. No man can be sued justly unless he has violated some law of Christ or departed from the spirit and design of Christianity. This is, at least, the case under the code of laws which governs our commercial intercourse in this country. But we do not suppose, nor teach, that only such cases of departure from the Christian institution as become cases of prosecution, are to be inquired into, or remonstrated against in a Christian congregation. No, indeed; every appearance of this evil spirit is to be guarded against as plague. No promise should be made, no covenant entered into, no obligation given, which is not to be held as sacred as a sacrament or an oath. When we hear of a Christian compelled to pay his debts by law, or to atone for the breach of covenants by fines; when we see one asking securities to obtain money on which to speculate, or see him eagerly engaged in the pursuit of wealth or any earthly distinctions, we must consider his conduct as great a libel on Christianity, as to see a college founded for the express purpose of aiding the cause of Christ, praying to the powers that be to allow it the privilege of not paying its debts, or of departing from its own engagements with impunity.

Every Christian's "Yea" should be "Yes," and his "Nay," "No." Every Christian's promise should be as inviolate as an oath, and all his engagements as sacred as his Christian profession. It is only when this is so, that persons will be cautious in entering into engagements, and punctual in living up to them. What a world of prevarication, double meaning, duplicity, circumvention, and lying, grow out of the latitudinarianism of these times. And when we trace all the bitterness, hard feelings, evil surmises, coldness of affection found in religious society, up to their proper source, we generally find they have originated either from the evils on which we descanted in our former essay, or from these of which we now treat. Punctuality in all engagements is an essential constituent of Christian morality. *"Owe no man anything but love,"* and *"Provide things honorable in the sight of all men,"* and *"Let our brethren learn to practice useful trades or the necessary uses,"* and many other apostolic injunctions which naturally flow from the religion of our Lord, make it necessary that Christian congregations should take these matters under their most serious consideration.

Nothing injures the cause of Christianity, nor retards its progress more, than the immortality of which we now speak. They are so visible, manifest, and so inimical to the political and temporal interests of society, that the children of this world, Deists, Atheists, and Sceptics of every name, are just as good judges of these questions, and can mark their progress and descant upon their effects with as much precision and fluency as Paul the Apostle could have done. They also pique themselves no little upon their superior attention to these matters. How lightly do they speak of the religion, the devotion, the praying, and religious gossiping of those who will not keep good faith, nor pay their debts, nor speak well of one another. This is the style in which they take off the edge of the reproofs and zeal of those who *profess* Christianity. After all their boast, their morality is a matter of policy and self-interest. Yet it is a political advantage, highly beneficial to society, and therefore its tendency most commendable. But without this a man's religion is vain. "For if a man does not know," says an Apostle, "how to bridle his own tongue, his religion is vain."

Every Christian congregation has, therefore, the best of reasons, as well as the highest authority, to induce them to take this matter under cognizance, and to make every departure from the letter and spirit of Christianity in these respects, a matter of discipline. On the discipline of such offences, we shall speak hereafter.

On the Discipline of the Church (No. V) [41]

They greatly mistake who expect to find a liturgy, or a code of laws in the New Institution, designed to govern Christians either in their private or public relations and character. This may be found in the Old Institution which the God of Abraham set

---

[41] "A Restoration of the Ancient Order of Things — No. XXVIII," *Christian Baptist* Vol. 6, No. 5 (1828).

up amongst the child of the flesh. The nation of the Jews affords both demonstration and proof that man cannot be governed or controlled either in piety or morality by any extrinsic law, however excellent or spiritual. The former institution was an institution of *law*—the new an institution of *favor*. Christians are not now, nor were they ever, under *law*, but under *favor*. Hence argues the Apostle: —"Sin shall not lord it over you; for you are *not under law* but *under favor.*" A single monosyllable represents the active principle, or law of subordination and of practical morality which it unfolds. That monosyllable is LOVE. *"Love is the fulfilling of the whole law."* The glad tidings of the divine philanthropy is the instrument or medium of the inspiration of this principle. The New Institution writes upon the *heart,* and not on *marble,* the governing principle, or laws of all religious and moral action. This truth recognized and apprehended, solves the difficulty which has puzzled so many minds, and so generally distracted religious society. Many Christians have read and rummaged the apostolic writings with the spirit and expectations of a Jew in perusing the writings of Moses-Jews in heart, but Christians in profession. They have sought, but sought in vain, for an express command or precedent for matters as minute as the seams in the sacerdotal robes, or the pins and pilasters of the tabernacle.

The remote or proximate causes of most errors in disciplinary proceedings may be traced either to the not perceiving that the distinguishing peculiarity of the New, or Christian Institution, is this—that it aims at governing human action without *letter,* and causes its votaries to "serve in newness of spirit, and not in the oldness of the letter;" or, to the not observing that the congregations which Christianity forms are designed rather as schools of moral excellence, than as courts of inquiry possessed of judicial authority.

To look still farther into the genius of the New Institution is yet prerequisite to just conclusions on this subject. The New Institution, governing religious and moral action by a law or principle engraved upon the heart, proposes certain acts of private and public edification and worship. These are stated in the apostolic writings, and conformity to them is enjoined upon disciples from the new obligations which arise out of the new law. The precepts found in the apostolic epistles and those found in the Pentateuch or writings of Moses, have one differential attribute which cannot be too clearly presented here. The precepts found in the apostolic epistles originated or were occasioned by the mistakes and misdemeanors found in Jews and Pagans, recently converted to the Christian faith. But the precepts of laws found in the Pentateuch were promulged before the people began to act at all, as a part of the institution itself. Hence it was an institution essentially of *law*—the New essentially an institution of *favor*. All the actions of the former were prescribed by law; but subordination to the latter is implied in the gracious promulgation itself.

The relation established between God and Israel was a different relation from that established between God and Christians. As all duties and privileges arise from relations, if the relations are different, the duties and privileges are different also. Now God made himself known to Israel simply as their God and deliverer from Egyptian bondage, and as their King in contradistinction from the kings of all other nations. Upon this fact as the grand premises, was the Old Institution proclaimed. Thus it began:—"I am the Lord your God who brought you out of the house of bondage. *Therefore* you shall acknowledge no other God besides me," etc. But the premises upon which the New Institution proceeds are of a much more sublime and exalted character. Relations more sublime than *national* and *temporal* relations, enter into its nature, and lay the foundation of the New Economy.

He is the God and King of Christians upon higher considerations—and more than simply their God and King—he is their Savior and Redeemer from worse than Egyptian bondage; their leader and guide to a better inheritance than Canaan; and their *Father* by a new and glorious provision which the national compact at Mount Sinai knew nothing of.

The relation of Master and Servant is a very different relation from that of Father and Son. This is rather an illustration, than a full representation of the difference of relation in which Jews and Christians stand to the God of the whole earth. The relation of Creator and creature is the natural relation existing between God and all mankind. But besides this he has instituted political and gracious relations between himself and human beings. These flow from his own good will and pleasure, and, as such, will be acquiesced in by the wise and good. The natural and first relation in which mankind stand to each other is that of *fellow-creatures;* but besides this, a number of other natural, political, and gracious relations have been either necessarily or graciously called into existence—such as that of parent and child, husband and wife, and the whole table of consanguinity and affinity; besides all the political relations, and those found in the kingdom of Jesus Christ.

Now the relation between God and Christians, or the relation which the New Institution develops, is the most gracious and desirable which can be conceived of; and therefore, presents to the human mind the loftiest and most comprehensive principles which can excite to moral action. As in physics, so in ethics there are principles or powers more influential than others. But Christianity discovers principles of action which no political, moral or religious relations hitherto known, could originate. These new relations, and these new principles of action, are stronger than death, more triumphant than the grave, and lasting as eternity. The discovery of a new, gracious, spiritual, and eternal relation, and correspondent principles of action, moral and religious, is the basis of that association called the Christian church or congregation. It is called the Reign or Kingdom of Heaven, because of the high and sublime nature of the relations, principles, duties, and privileges which it develops. All the political, commercial, and temporal relations of what nature or kind soever, which human passions, interests, partialities, or antipathies have given rise to, are weak and transient as the spider's thread compared with these. Hence the superlative glory of the New Institution. The world knows it not. It knew not the founder, and it apprehends not the institution. The light shines in darkness, but the darkness reaches it not.

These premises merely stated, not illustrated, suggest the true reason why, in the discipline of the church, so much is to be done before a member is to be severed from her embraces, In the politico-ecclesiastical relations of schismatic corporations the ties of consociation are neither very binding, nor the relations very endearing. They are not much stronger than the purse strings of the treasurer, nor more durable than the paper on which is written the shibboleth of their Magna Charta. Members may be, and often are, separated without a pang or a sorrow. There is none of that tenderness of reproof, of correction, of admonition, of dehortations, of persuasion, known in such confederations as that which the New Institution enjoins upon the citizens of Heaven.

The first effort which the genius of the New Institution enjoins with respect to offending brothers, is similar to that notable regulation concerning private trespasses, which, all who have read it, remembers, aims at *gaining* the supposed aggressor or delinquent. Hence the most characteristic feature in all congregational proceedings in reference to those who sin, not so much against a brother as against Christ, is that condescending tenderness which aims at the conversion of the delinquent or transgressor. The dernier resort, when all means fail, is separation. This tender solicitude and earnestness to *gain a brother* who has fallen, is, in some cases, where the nature of the case does not forbid, extended even beyond exclusion. So that although public good as well as that of the subject of censure, does require his exclusion; yet even then he is not to be treated as an enemy, but admonished as a brother. The lesson of all others the most difficult, and the most important to be learned on the subject of this essay, is that which the preceding considerations suggest, and that is briefly that every part of the proceedings in reference to an offending brother must be distinguished by every possible demonstration of sympathy and concern for his good standing and character in the sight of God and man: and that final seclusion from the congregation must not be attempted until admonition, reproof, and persuasion have failed to effect a real change in his views and behavior. Though I neither hold Lord Chesterfield nor his writings in much esteem, yet I cannot but admire his happy use of the *"suaviter in modo"*[42] and the *"fortiter in re,"*[43] so much commended in his letters. If the *"suaviter in modo,"* or the sweetness or gracefulness in the *manner of doing,* could always accompany the *"fortiter in re,"* or the *firmness in the purpose,* or in *the thing to* be *done,* it would be no less useful than ornamental even amongst Christians in all their congregational proceedings relating to offenders.

On the Discipline of the Church (No. V): Continued [44]

In the preceding essays under this head, we have paid some attention to the nature of *private* and *public offences,* and to some

---

[42] Or, "pleasant in manner."
[43] Or, "powerful in deed."
[44] "Discipline of the Church — No. V," *Christian Baptist* Vol. 6, No. 6 (1829).

of the general principles which are to be regarded in our treatment of them. We have also had occasion to call up to the attention of our readers some prevailing defects in the morality of Christians which are not generally taken cognizance of in any of the modern establishments. In our last we spoke of the deep solicitude for the restoration of a delinquent, and long continued forbearance which Christians are to exhibit towards him, for his ultimate recovery from the snare of the wicked one. But, while recommending to the consideration of our brethren the Christian propriety and expediency of exercising much long suffering towards transgressors, and all mildness in our efforts to reclaim them from the error of their way, we must imitate the conduct of one, who while attempting to pull another out of the fire, has to use the greatest caution lest the flame seize his own garments. Jude says, "Have compassion, indeed, on some transgressors; but others save by fear snatching them out of the fire; hating even the garment spotted by the flesh." There is to be no conformity to the obliquity of the transgressor to reclaim him. We are not to drink a little with the drunkard, nor to tattle a little with the tattler nor to detract with the slanderer, in order to convert them from the error of their way. While we show all tenderness for their persons, and all solicitude for their complete and perpetual felicity, we are not to show the least partiality for their faults, or a disposition to diminish aught from the malignity of their trespasses. We ought to lay their sins before them in all their true colors, without extenuation or apology; while we beseech and entreat them to abandon every sinful and pernicious way. There is often too much care taken to diminish from, and make excuses for, an immoral or unchristian act. Hence, we cheapen offence in the eyes of those who were wont to regard it in a much more heinous point of view. To show all willingness to restore him that is overtaken in a fault, and at the same time to exhibit the most unmingled detestation of the fault, crime, or whatever it may be called, is just the point to be gained by all those who aspire to the character of perfect men in Christ Jesus.

Indeed, there cannot be too much circumspection exercised over the conduct of all those with whom we fraternize in the kingdom of Jesus. Many of those in all countries who profess the Christian religion, are extremely ignorant of the dignity of their profession, and they are too familiar with the low, mean, and demoralizing converse of the world. Many of them, too, are altogether uncultivated in their minds and manners, and so completely enchased in penury and ignorance, as to preclude the hope of much mental enlargement or improvement, except from the sheer influences of reading and hearing the oracles of God. Christianity can, and does, impart a real dignity and elevation to all who cordially embrace it. The poor and the unlettered become not only *tolerable* but *agreeable* members of the Christian community; and while they are commanded to rejoice in that they are exalted, the rich and the learned in this world who rejoice in that they are made low, can most cordially congratulate them on their promotion to the rank of sons of God. But there must not be, for, indeed, there cannot be, any insolence or haughtiness amongst those who are all made *one* in the kingdom of Jesus, arising from any of the relations which exist in the frame and government of this world. The virtuous, poor, and unlettered Christian, who is walking in truth, is just as honorable and exalted in the estimation of all the inhabitants of the upper world, as those who, from circumstances beyond their creation, have ranked higher and been more adored by a mistaken and ill-judging world. Piety and pure morality constitute the only nobility in the kingdom of heaven.

It is, too, a happy circumstance in the original development and exhibition of Christianity, which must eternally echo the praise of its founder, that the scene of its perfecting purity is laid rather below, than at, or above mediocrity, as respects all earth-born distinction. While but a few of the rich, the learned, and the noble, were honored with a place amongst the heirs of immortality, the poor and the unlettered constituted not only the great mass of the army of the faithful; but all the captains, commanders, generals, and chiefs were of the most common class of society. So that the history and biography of the New Testament present the most astonishing spectacle ever seen before — the poorest and most illiterate of men, shining in wisdom and purity, which cast into an eternal shade the wisdom and morality of all the sages and moralists of the Pagan world. It thus adapts itself to the great mass of society and proves its superlative excellence in giving a moral polish and luster to that great body of men which all other systems had proved ineffectual to renovate, to improve, or even to restrain.

Now this great improvement is not the effect of good laws, but of good examples. No system of policy, no code of laws could have at first effected it or can affect it now. The living model of the glorious chief, the living example of his immediate disciples, and the example of the disciples in their associated capacity, give the first impulse. The continued watchfulness of the brotherhood and their affectionate regard for the welfare of one another, operate like the laws of attraction in the material system. But not only the happiness of the society, but also its usefulness in the world, depend chiefly upon this care and watchfulness of the members of the body, one over and for another. Nothing has ever given so much weight to the Christian arguments as the congenial lives of those who profess it. On the other hand, nothing has defeated the all-subduing plea of speculative Christianity (as it may be called) so much as the discordant lives of these who profess to believe it. Had it not been for this one drawback, Christianity this day had known no limits on this side of the most distant home of man.

Now we must admit that in no age, the primitive age of Christianity not excepted, have all who have professed it acted up to its requirements. Many have apostatized from its profession altogether, and many who have not acted so flagitiously as to exclude them from the *name,* have, even in the estimation of their own friends, forfeited the *character* of real believers, Paul wept over the lives of such professors, and deplored their profession as more inimical to the doctrine of the cross than the avowed hostility of the open enemies of Christianity. The hardened sceptic (for such there are who hate the light) rejoices over the flaws and blemishes of Christians as the shamble fly over the putrid specks in the dead carcass. He feasts and fattens in his infidelity upon the moral corruptions of those who, in deeds, deny the Savior. And as the heavenly messengers rejoice more over one sinner that reforms, than over ninety-nine just persons who need no reformation; so he rejoices more over one Christian that apostatizes, than over the wickedness of ninety-nine profligates who never professed the faith. Now as a real Christian would be the last in theory or in practice to afford him such a feast, so let every Christian watch over his brethren, that none of them may either comfort the wicked or afflict the saints — that none of them may encourage the unbelieving, or cause the faithful to drop a tear over his fall.

So long as a man evidently desires to please Christ, whatever we may think of his opinions, we are to love his as a brother. But when he evidently departs from his law, and tramples upon the authority of the Great King, we must exclude him.

There are some who talk of *forgiving* their brethren when they transgress. This is a mode of expression which is to be used with great caution. When a brother trespasses against a brother, he that has received the injury may, and ought to forgive the injurious, when he acknowledges his fault. But when a man publicly offends against Christ, (for example, gets drunk,) his brethren cannot *forgive* him. There is no such power lodged in their hands. How then are they to be reconciled to him as a brother, and receive him as such? When they believe or have reason to believe that God has forgiven him. But how is this to be ascertained? When any Christian has been overtaken in a fault, repents of it, confesses it, and asks forgiveness for it, we have reason to believe that he is pardoned. "For if we confess our sins, he is faithful and just to forgive us our sins; and the blood of Jesus Christ, his Son, cleanses us from all sin." Whenever, we have reason to believe that our Heavenly Father has forgiven our brother, we cannot avoid forgiving him and receiving him, because God has received him. And if he has kindly and graciously received him, how much more we, who are also polluted, and in the same hazard of falling while in the body. This, then, is the rule and reason in all disciplinary proceedings against offenders: —When their penitence is so manifest as to authorize us to consider them as received into the kingdom of God, we must receive them into our favor, and treat them as though they had not transgressed. And here it may be observed, that the more frequently a brother transgresses, it will be the more difficult for us to know that he has repented; and it may be so often as to preclude, in ordinary cases, all hope of his restoration. But before there has been any fall, it is much easier to prevent them to restore; and therefore, in all Christian congregations, prayer for one another, and watchfulness, with all love and tenderness, will, than all other means do more to prevent faults and fallings in our brethren.

On the Discipline of the Church (No. VI) [45]

While on the subject of discipline, we wished to have been more methodical; but causes and circumstances, too tedious to detail, have compelled us to break through our method, and to become immethodical. The subject of the present essay is forced upon us from some incidents of recent and remote occurrence. A writer in the *Religious Herald,* under the name and character of *Herodion,* in December last, discusses the following question "Does the expulsion of a member from an individual church of the Baptist faith and order, exclude him from fellowship with the whole denomination." If I correctly understand *Herodion,* he answers in the *affirmative.* The editor of the *Religious Herald* dissents from *Herodion* in this decision. The former will have the Association the sovereign arbiter-the latter would make his appeal to a co-ordinate or sister church. But to make out a case in point for illustrating this question, we shall introduce that of Titus Timothy. —Titus Timothy was a regular Baptist, but somehow took it into his head that it was not right in a Christian church to receive or retain slaveholders. The church to which he belonged thought otherwise. And for his impertinence in advocating this matter and dissenting from his brethren, they excluded him. Now Titus found himself cast out of the church. He did not like it, to be sure. But what could he do? He referred his case to *Herodion. Herodion* told him to "pray to God for redress, and to wait for a change of temper in his oppressors." He prayed and waited for a long time. No change took place in his favor. He went to my friend, the *Religious Herald.* He advised him to "appeal to a co-ordinate church." But thinking in the multitude

[45] "Discipline of the Church—No. VI," *Christian Baptist* Vol. 6, No. 8 (1829).

of counsellors there was safety, he went back to *Herodion. Herodion* told him to "appeal to the Association." As *Herodion* was older and more experienced than his brother of the *Herald,* he took his advice, and appealed to the Association. He made his appeal. But alas! In vain! For the Association told him they had no power to overrule the decision of the church, for this would be to divest it of its independence. Titus was worse hurt than before: for now he found that the decision of the church was confirmed by the Association without seeming to take it into consideration; for by throwing him and his case out of doors, they indirectly confirmed the decision of the church. They retained it and excluded him. He went back to the *Religious* Herald — told over his case. His appeal to the Association was disapproved; and now, as the case stands, he is advised to call a council of helps from the neighboring churches. He does so. But the church which excluded him refuses to attend, or to admit of such interference. The council cannot act upon *exparte* testimony, and he is still excluded from the whole denomination. The two neighboring churches enter complaint at the next Association against the church for intolerance, and despite of an *advisory council.* The excluding church, by her delegates, protests against the conduct of the two neighboring churches for presuming to complain of her upon *exparte* testimony and argues her independence. So, the affair ends, and poor Titus Timothy is at his wit's end. He is excluded from the whole denomination for *thinking wrong,* or rather for uttering his thoughts.

But another case presents itself. *Stephen Seektruth* was a member of a church composed of eighteen members, six males and twelve females. He read the New Institution with great attention and unfeigned devotion. He was persuaded that the church was unsupported in her resolve to meet only once a month in her *official capacity.* He remonstrated, and, for insubordination to the brotherhood, was expelled. Four of the sisters were absent when

189

the final vote was taken. Two of the brethren and five of the sisters voted for, and three of the brethren and three of the sisters voted against his exclusion. So that the voice of a single sister cast him out of the assembly. He appealed to the Association, but they would not hear any individual. Consequently, they confirmed the decision of the church, and Stephen was in fact excluded from the whole Baptist denomination by the vote of a woman! He was advised to call for helps from other churches, but they would not meet on the complaint of the *injured:* and the *injurers* would not submit to be arraigned before any such tribunal. Under the opprobrium of an excluded member, he must live and die.

Sects and *denominations* require modes of governments adapted to their genius. Romanists must have a pope in one man; the good old Episcopalians must have a king, and archbishops, and all the army of subalterns; the Presbyterians must have synods and a general assembly; and the good old English Baptists must have associations. Without these the *denominations* would be broken down, and might, perhaps, become Christians of the old stamp. But each of these denominations require all the sectarian machinery to keep them in a thriving sectarian spirit. The Baptist system, we have always said and seen, is the most impotent of any of them. They have, *in theory,* sawed the horns off the Beast, and the Association is a hornless stag, with the same ferocious spirit which he had when the horns were on his head. If he is offended, he makes a tremendous push with his brains, and *bruises* to death the obnoxious carcass which he would have *gored* clear through at a single push, if he had his horns. *Herodion* feels the want of horns and would have the creature furnished with at least one artificial one, which he might occasionally use. My brother of the *Herald* would wish to feed the stag well but would still be sawing off the horns: perhaps I may wrong him in so saying, for indeed he is very modest about

190

it. But, for my part, I do not love even an *Image* of the Beast. I have no objection to congregations meeting in hundreds, at stated times, *to sing God's praise,* and to unite their prayers and exhortations for the social good. But whenever they form a quorum, and call for the business of the churches, they are a popish calf, or *muley,* or a hornless stag, or something akin to the old grand Beast with seven heads and *ten* horns.

I cannot give my voice in favor of *appeals* to any tribunal, but to the congregation of which the offended is a member; neither to a council of churches specially called, nor to an association. The old book, written by the Apostles, has compelled me to hold this dogma fast. And I can, I know, show that it is superior to every other course. I will grant, however, that this plan will not suit a *denomination* or a *sect;* but it will suit the kingdom over which *Immanuel* reigns. And neither *Herodion,* nor any other brother of more or less experience, can support his scheme from the statute book of the Great King. But if he should think so, let him try, and I will try to make my assertion good. But I do pity such good old men. They have borne the burden and heat of the day in maintaining a denomination scheme, and to suspect now that they have not fought in the ranks of the good old martyrs, is a terrible thought to an honest and Lord-loving and fearing spirit. My hopes are in the young men who are now entering the field. And I know some hundred of them just now who are likely to die good soldiers of Jesus Christ. The friends of the ancient order would be too elated, perhaps, and its opposers would be too disconsolate, if they knew the forces now commencing and commenced their operations. I do not care for offending a *coward.* He will only fight when there is no danger. And a time-serving spirit I would rather see on the opposite side: for he will fight most stoutly for them who pay him best. We want men in the spirit and power of Elijah, who would tell a king Herod to his face that he was a transgressor. It cost the first *Baptist* his head, to be sure. But what of that? He will not want a head in the resurrection! O! for some *Baptists* of the good old stamp! Not the Kentucky *old stamp* of the Oakley school. But whither have I been driven? To the point: Every Christian community must settle its own troubles. No appeal from one congregation to another. There is no need of it; for no intelligent Christian congregation will ever cast out a person who could be an honor to any community. This much at present on this topic; but more hereafter.

Here a friend tells me I have mistaken the question; for Paul taught the Corinthians to appeal to a sister church. "See," says he, "1 Corinthians 7 where Paul says, 'Brethren, ye greatly err: when any one troubleth you, and when disputations arise among you, call for helps from the churches of Macedonia: let the disputers be brought face to face; and when the pleaders on each side have impleaded each other, then do ye call for the votes of the brotherhood. If there is only one of a majority, cast him out; for as Moses saith in the Law, "The majority is always right."' But if any thinketh that he is not fairly cast out, or that there is not a real majority against him, let him appeal to the whole Macedonian association, and let them judge the case. If the majority of the Macedonian association cast him or them out, then let them be stigmatized by all the associations in Greece. For I would have you, brethren, to mark out the heretics and the disturbers of the brethren, and therefore, publish them in your Minutes, that all the churches on earth may be apprised of the ungodly.

On the Discipline of the Church (No. VII) [46]

Queries for the Christian Baptist – Continued

Query 25. —Should a member be excluded from a Christian church, who only, once in a while, attends the meeting of the brethren; when, in other respects, his conduct is orderly?

Answer. – We are not aware of the importance of the question unless we form a correct view of the nature of the Christian institution. Amongst some sects, and in some churches, they have agreed to meet once a fortnight, or once a month, and only require their members thus periodically to assemble. They censure those who depart from the covenant of the church, or those who do not assemble twelve or twenty-four times a year. But the Head and Founder of the Christian religion disclaims both the covenant and practice of such assemblies. The covenant and the practice are in direct contravention of his authority and design. If then, the whole church meets once a month, faithfully and fully according to the covenant, they are in a sort of mutiny against the Captain, or in a state of rebellion against the King. For they have neither his promises, blessing, nor presence, when they wittingly and cordially agree to neglect the weekly assembling of themselves together. They might as scripturally expect his countenance, blessing and presence, should they agree to one annual or semi-annual meeting during their lives. The platform, as well as the practice, is anti-scriptural. And I do not see why a church who agrees to meet once a month, should censure any member who will only visit them once a year. The same license

---

[46] "A Restoration of the Ancient Order of Things — No. XXIX," *Christian Baptist* Vol. 6, No. 10 (1829).

for transgressing, which they claim for themselves, will equally tolerate him. But, I think, this matter is clearly proved in the preceding volumes of this work, if anything is proved in it, namely, that the whole system of monthly meetings for business and to hear a text explained, is as foreign from the Christian institutes as transubstantiation, consubstantiation, Christmas, or Easter carnivals. Viewing, as I do, the custom of assembling monthly for business and preaching, to be a branch from the same root from which spring Lent, Easter, Christmas, Whitsunday, and Good Friday. I could not blame the delinquent more than the observer of this tradition of the fathers. But where an assembly, constituted upon the traditions of the Apostles, agree to meet every Lord's Day, the person who willingly, for weeks forsakes the assembling of the saints, is on the high road to apostacy. This Paul avows by his connecting with exhortation to perseverance, and dehortations against apostacy, his remonstrance against forsaking the assembling of themselves together. No person who detaches himself from a Christian assembly for his ease or any worldly concern, can deserve the confidence of his brethren, any more than a wife who deserts the bed and board of her husband, or a child who, in his minority, deserts the table and fireside of his father and mother, can deserve the confidence and affection of those relatives they have forsaken. Nor can a church consistently regard and treat as brethren those who do not frequent their stated solemnities. Such absentees are to be dealt with as other offenders; and if reformation be not the result, they are as worthy of exclusion as other transgressors. Demas was as much of an apostate as Hymenaeus and Philetus.

Few Christians seem to appreciate the wisdom and benevolence of the Great Founder of the Christian institution exhibited most impressively in this instance, in laying the disciples under the blissful necessity and obligation of keeping up a spirited social intercourse. The grand design of the Christian institution is to draw us to a common center, in approaching which we approximate towards each other in every step. Thus, with the great fountain of life and happiness in view, in soaring to it we are necessarily elevated together above earthly influences and drawn together by ties and considerations which draw all hearts and hands to the throne of the Eternal. Now the Christian institution is the most social thing under the heavens — but to substitute hearing the same sermon, subscribing the same covenant, and going to the same meeting place, in lieu of the social institutions of the kingdom of heaven, is to substitute a spider's thread for a cable to retain a ship to her anchorage during a tempest. Nothing is more unlike the Christian kingdom than the dry, cold formalities which appear in the inside of a Baptist or Presbyterian meeting house. The order within the walls is as near to the order of that house over which the Son of God presides; "whose house are we, if we hold fast our begun confidence unshaken to the end."

Men depart as far from nature as they do from Christianity in conforming to the regulations of the *Geneva* school. The doctrine is as cold as moonshine, and the initiated in their arrangements and order are like so many icicles hanging to the eaves of a house in a winter's morning, clear, cold, formal, in rank and file; but they will break rather than bend towards each other. A tree frog is generally the color of the timber, rail, or fence on which it is found. So are the Baptists. They are, in these regions, generally the offspring, or converts from the Presbyterian ranks, and they wear the same visage in their order, except with this small difference, that the Baptists build their meeting houses near ponds or rivers, while the Presbyterians build theirs on the tops of the hills.

But were Christians to get into the spirit of the institution of the Great *Philanthropist,* they would have as much relish for the weekly meeting in honor of the resurrection of their chief, and in anticipation of their own, as the stranger has for the sweet word *home*. But so long as like the Jews they meet in memory of the reason assigned in the fourth commandment, or by an act of congress, they will have nothing to fire their zeal, kindle their love, animate their strains, or enlarge their hopes. And as demure and silent as Quakers, except when the parson, who has a plenary inspiration, is present, they will sit or stand, as the case may be, until they hear the sermon, and all the appurtenances thereunto belonging. Now if such persons were to be translated into an old-fashioned Christian assembly, they would be as much astonished with the natural simplicity, affection, and piety of the worshippers, as a blind man would be on the recovery of his sight.

To return to the point—Were a member of a family to be missing from table ten times a week, or twice a day, would we not at last inquire for his health or cause of his absence, and visit him accordingly? Most certainly we would. Why not then exhibit the same concern for a member of Christ's family? Absence from the table always exhibits a want of appetite, or some more pressing call. On either hypothesis, when a member is missing, it deserves inquiry—and when the true cause is ascertained, it demands a suitable treatment. But that stiffness and formality which are now the mode, and the want of due regard to the nature, design, and authority of every part of the Christian institution, lead us into a practice alike repugnant to reason and revelation.

Query 26—Should the majority govern in all cases, or should unanimity be considered indispensable in all matters which come before the church? —[*Indiana*.]

Answer. —Carrying matters by a numerical force, or by a majority of votes, is very natural under popular governments. And as the Baptists have very generally been republicans in politics, they are republicans in ecclesiastics. And, indeed, in all matters of a temporal nature, there seems to be no other way of deciding. Yet it does not well consort with the genius of Christianity to carry a point by a majority. Where the law and testimony are either silent or not very explicit upon any question, reason says that we ought not to be either positive of dictatorial. There are but some hints and allusions to be found in the New Testament on this subject. Perhaps the reason is, that the churches set in order by the Apostles had not much occasion for the resolution of such queries. There was not so much left to their decision, as, in our superior sagacity, we have found necessary. As the government was on the shoulders of the Great King, the church had not so much to do with it as we moderns imagine. Some things, it is true, are left to the brethren, such as the reception of members, the selection of persons to offices, and the arrangements which are purely secular. The former in their nature requires unanimity — the latter may dispense with a majority. In receiving a member, he must be received by all, for all are to love and treat him as a brother. In selecting a person to an office, such as the bishops, deacons, or that of a messenger, there is not the same necessity; yet a near approach to unanimity is absolutely necessary, and if attainable, is much to be preferred. But in matters purely *secular*, such as belong to the place of meeting, and all the prerequisites, circumstances, and adjuncts, there is not the same necessity for a full unanimity. To require unanimity in all questions which we moderns bring into our churches, is to require an impossibility. But in secular affairs, in the primitive church, what we call a committee, or arbitrators, were chosen, and some of the questions which we submit to the brotherhood were submitted to the rulers or bishops. Take out of the church's business what the ancients referred to a committee, and what belonged to the bishops, there is not so much left to quarrel about. The overseers or rulers were only in such matters executors of the law of the sovereign authority. When a man was proved to be a drunkard, or a reviler, or a fornicator, it was not to be submitted to the vote of the brotherhood whether he ought to be expelled. When a man came forward and was born of water or immersed into the faith in the presence of a church, it was not to be decided by a vote whether he should be received into the society. When a child is born into a family, it is not to be voted whether it shall be received into it. It is true that when a man is born into the kingdom of heaven, it may be necessary for him to apply, and to be received into some particular congregation, in which he is to .be enrolled, and in fellowship with which he is to walk; and then he must be unanimously received. But it is worthy of remark that a large share of brotherly love, and the not laying an undue stress upon a perfect unanimity will be more productive of it than we are aware of, and the more it is sought after in a contrary spirit, the more difficult it will be to obtain.

Chapter Eighteen

Official Names and Titles [47]

The religious theatre of public actors is crowded. To find suitable names to designate them all would be a desideratum. We have Ministers, Divines, Clergymen, Elders, Bishops, Preachers, Teachers, Priests, Deans, Prebendaries, Deacons, Archbishops, Archdeacons, Cardinals, Popes, Friars, Priors, Abbots, Local Preachers, Circuit Preachers, Presiding Elders, Missionaries, Class Leaders, Licentiates, *cum multis aliis.*[48] I do not know what to do with them all. I would call them all by scriptural names if I could find them. But it is very difficult to find scriptural names for unscriptural things.

I have rummaged the inspired books to find some scriptural names for them all, or some general names, under which, with some sort of affinity, we might hope to class them. But this is also a difficult task. I find the following are the nearest approach I can make: —Deacons, Bishops, Preachers, Evangelists, Antichrists. This last term is a sort of *summum genus*[49] for a large majority of them. The term *preacher* will hardly apply to any of them, in its scriptural import. Christian *mothers* who make known to their children the glad tidings, or the facts concerning the Savior, are the worthiest of this name than any persons now on earth. Evangelists will not strictly apply to any, in its primitive usage. Though the *printers* of the history of Jesus Christ, and those who proclaim the ancient gospel, in the capacity of public

---

[47] "A Restoration of the Ancient Order of Things — No. XXX," *Christian Baptist* Vol. 7, No. 2 (1829).

[48] Or, "with many other matters."

[49] Or, "the highest genus," which cannot be categorized under as a species of any other genus.

speakers, may, of all others, deserve to inherit this name with the most reasonable pretensions. *Elders* will apply to old men, only, whether they are official or unofficial members of society. *Overseers* or *Bishops* will apply to all, and to none but those who have the presidency or oversight of one congregation. *Deacons,* to those males who are the public servants of the whole congregation. *Deaconesses,* to those female public servants, who officiate amongst the females. *Teacher,* is a generic term which will then apply to all men in the capacity of public instructors. As for the others, I cannot classify them. The word *antichrist* covers a goodly number of them; and it is not worth the labor to tell which of them may escape the enrollment. They who have more leisure may amuse themselves with such speculations.

The officers of the Christian congregations found in the *New Institution* were *overseers* and *public servants,* or *bishops and deacons.*—Every well-ordered congregation was supplied with these. They had one, or more, male and female deacons, who served the congregations in performing such service or ministry to the male and female members of their respective communities, as circumstances required; but all these official duties were confined to one single congregation. Such a thing as a bishop over two, three, or four congregations, was as unknown, unheard of, and unthought of in the primitive and ancient order of things in the Christian communities, as a husband with two, three, or four living wives. There is just as much reason and scripture for one pope and twelve cardinals, as for one bishop and four congregations.

A *bittersweet* or a *sweet bitter* is not more incongruous than a *young elder,* or to see a young stripling addressed as an elder. It is not long since I saw, in a newspaper, such an annunciation as this: "Elder A.B. will preach at such a place at such an hour." But the satire was that *elder* A.B. was not *twenty-three* years old. Another equally incongruous was, that "bishop W.T. will lecture in the courthouse on the first Sunday of July." The humor was that *bishop* W.T. had no diocese, nor cure, nor see, nor congregation, nor oversight on this side of the moon. Now, what shall we do with these anomalies? I answer, call no man a *bishop* or overseer, who has not a flock or an oversight; call no man a *deacon* who is not the public servant of a community; call those who proclaim the ancient gospel *evangelists*.

This, upon the whole, is the least exceptionable name for them. It does, in its etymology, just express the proclamation of the glad tidings; and if it did not import anything more, it cannot now. The ancients called those who *wrote* as well as those who *spoke* the facts constituting the gospel history, by this name. Besides, the office of evangelist, as a proclaimer of the gospel, was always contingent. He was needed only in some places, and at some times, and was not a permanent officer of the Christian church. His office *now* answers to that of the prophets of old. The prophets as extemporaneous and occasional teachers became necessary. When then, any congregation has a brother well qualified to proclaim the gospel, and when there is, in the vicinity, a people in need of such a service, let the person so sent by them, be called an *evangelist*. Perhaps the present distress requires such persons as much as any former period. But when Christian congregations cover the country and walk in the instituted order of the new constitution, such persons will not be necessary, any more than a standing army in time of peace.

But when we speak of the armies of the *sects*, how shall we denominate them? Let us call them all *teachers* of their respective tenets; such as teacher of Methodism, teacher of Presbyterianism; or Independent teachers, Baptist teachers, Methodist teachers, etc. This is not at all disrespectful nor incongruous. In addressing letters, or in publishing the names and offices of persons, in order to save time, paper, and ink, let us use the following abbreviations: Bp. for *bishop*, Dn. for *deacon*, Et. for *Evangelist*.

Distinctions of this sort are only necessary for discrimination from persons of similar names in the same vicinities. There is a great love in the American people for titles. So strong is this passion that many retain the title of an office, which, perhaps, they only filled a year or two, all their lives. How many captains, majors, colonels, generals, esquires, have we who have become obsolete. Christians cannot, consistently with their profession, desire the official name without the *work*. If a man, says Paul, desire the office of a bishop, he desires a good *work*. The *work* then and not the *name* or title engrosses the ambition of the Christian.

In the common intercourse of life, it is requisite that we give all their dues. Even where honor is due, the debt ought to be paid. Paul thought it no incongruity with the Christian apostleship to call a *Pagan governor "Most noble Felix."* This very term Luke, the amiable physician, and evangelist, applies to a Christian brother of high political standing, *"most noble Theophilus."* We ought to address all men wearing official titles, when we address them publicly, by the titles which designate their standing among men. There is a squeamishness of conscience, or a fastidiousness of taste, which some men, and some sectaries exhibit about giving any official names or titles to men of high rank or standing. This proceeds more from pride than from humility, and more from the intimation of some eccentric genius than from the examples of either patriarchs, prophets, saints, or martyrs in the age of God's revelations. Let us then endeavor to call things by their proper names; and render to all men their dues.

www.ingramcontent.com/pod-product-compliance
Lightning Source LLC
LaVergne TN
LVHW051232080426
835513LV00016B/1547